AN EPISTLE TO THE APOSTLES IN THE MARKETPLACE

AROME OSAYI

AN EPISTLE TO THE APOSTLES IN THE MARKETPLACE

Copyright © August 2020 by **Arome Osayi**

ISBN: 978-978-971-882-5

Published in The Federal Republic of Nigeria by:
IRON PEN KALMA KRAFT LTD
Beside Shabu Development Area Secretariat,
Lafia, Nasarawa State.
ironpenpublishing@gmail.com
08033569841

All rights reserved.
No portion of this book may be used without the written permission of the publisher, with the exception of articles, brief excerpts, critical reviews, etc.

Unless otherwise indicated, all Scripture quotations are taken from the King James Version of the Bible (NKJV).

Scripture quotations marked (NKJV), (NIV), and (AMP) are taken from the New King James Version, New International Version and The Amplified Bible respectively.

Contents

Introduction.. iv
Acknowledgements vii
Dedication ix

CHAPTER 1: Dear Apostle in the Marketplace 1
CHAPTER 2: The Marketplace of Nations.......................... 16
CHAPTER 3: Egypt And Babylon: The Twin Platforms Of The Marketplace........... 43
CHAPTER 4: Spiritstorm.. 71
CHAPTER 5: Strike And Spare Not...................................... 99
CHAPTER 6: Build With Stones And Not Bricks 115
CHAPTER 7: Between Caesar And God 126
CHAPTER 8: Grace And Diligence 144
CHAPTER 9: The Lord's Cup And The Cup Of Devils 160
CHAPTER 10: The Goal Is Souls, The Means Is Gold 167
CHAPTER 11: Righteous Stewardship 182
CHAPTER 12: You Are Not Outnumbered: The Majority Of One With God! 196

Introduction

Suddenly it has become very clear to the whole world that no matter how seemingly impregnable systems are, as long as they have been created by man's hands, they are vulnerable to the incessant instabilities that couch violently in the four corners of the earth. It also proves beyond every reasonable doubt that there is no security under heaven; there are just opportunities. The most secure place to be is, therefore, in Christ!

Within the earth's wobbly four corners sits the world, comprised of nations of all kinds. There is a transcultural, transcontinental and eclectic intersection among nations that facilitates trade, commerce, industry, immigration, emigration, innovation, and the very expansion of the frontiers of human civilisation. This is called the *marketplace of nations* which the author has sufficiently explained is primarily made up of economy and government.

As this age draws to a close, persecutions and tribulations will increase geometrically, but so will opportunities for scaling up the preaching of the kingdom of our Lord Jesus reach colossal proportions. The fields of the world are white and ready - nations are overly ripe for harvesting. It is time for a new kind of apostles to arise from the four corners of the church and get deployed to harness and make the most of this global harvest. The job of establishing and extending the frontiers of the

INTRODUCTION

kingdom of heaven in the marketplace will not be done in the church; it will be done boots-on-the-ground by apostles specially called to dominate the marketplace of nations. These apostles' task is simple: glorify Christ and extinguish darkness in all its hues and nuances.

This apostolic army consists of artisans, hair dressers, tailors, bankers, engineers, pilots, politicians, plumbers, doctors, janitors, security guards, civil servants, drivers, traders, farmers, etc. With all these hands on deck, it is inevitable that the gates of hell will suffer huge wreck in righteousness!

This book is fitting because it was forged at the behest of the Timeless One. It is a condensed testimony of two decades of intense apostleship both in the body of Christ and in the marketplace. It is not the concoction of closeted research – it is the by-product of obedience and immense experience in the marketplace by God's servant, Arome Osayi.

The timeliness of this work was consolidated when shortly after it was completed early in 2020, the COVID-19 Pandemic took the world by storm. And the world still gasps under its chokehold as the economies and governments of nations grapple with mammoth consternation. The global lockdown has indisputably brought to the fore the need to reinforce and emphasise the importance of the apostles in the marketplace of nations. Again, the harvest is not in the church; it is in the world. It is time the church of the living God started redirecting the labour traffic and glut within her walls to the marketplace of nations.

INTRODUCTION

The message of this masterpiece is simple: It is time for all the Lord's apostles in the marketplace of the nations to arise and put the sickle in!

Rabeeu Nas Madaki
August, 2020
LAFIA, NIGERIA

Acknowledgements

Each time we embark on a book project, we know a lot is at stake in heaven and earth. The gestation period is usually very intense as we keep our hearts tethered to God's heart to ensure a seamless transfer of His word and burden for our generation. Despite the tremendous toll this takes on us, it remains a great honour to be chosen by Him to publish His word.

I thank the Lord for the blessing of a compact and spiritually intelligent team that keeps making this possible. I could not wish for a better bunch. It breaks my heart each time I have to do this: mention only a few by name because of the paucity of space and keep the rest baptised in the blessing of the apostolic mandate the Lord has given us. My only consolation is that the Lord who sees in the secret has not stopped rewarding openly!

I thank my darling wife, Dinna, for the great support and sacrifice, for keeping the home front annexed to heaven. Her partnership and loyalty are worth more than gold. She is not only someone I share the covenant of matrimony with; she is my number one confidante! I thank my children, Joshua and Esther, for sacrificing so much in keeping up with my ever-expanding labours in the gospel of the kingdom of our Lord Jesus Christ. I do not take any of this for granted. I love you guys profoundly.

I thank my father in the faith, Dr John E. Akpami, for his depth of wisdom, precious oversight and fatherly companionship. His legacy to me in the gospel is very evident for all to see. Daddy, the

ACKNOWLEDGEMENTS

Lord Himself is your reward.

I thank my dear friend and covenant brother, Gideon Odoma, for taking time out of his hectic schedule to make this work editorially solid and for granting us permission to use one of his many great pieces. His selflessness is only matched by His love for Jesus. Thank you so much, sir.

I thank the publishing team at Iron Pen Kalma Kraft Ltd. for developing the manuscript and coordinating the production of this book. Only the Lord Himself is your limit!

I thank my Remnant Christian Family for giving their all to ensure the mandate to *Strive for the Rebirth of Apostolic Christianity* is now a global phenomenon. The recent global upsurge has only been made possible because you guys first believed in the word of God in my mouth and lent me your ears and hearts to make full proof of the ministry. You guys are the best.

I thank you, the reader, for being with us from day one. May the Lord initiate the much-needed apostolic paradigm shift in your life as you dig into this piece and connect with the ageless wisdom of Zion's Great Monarch!

Dedication

This book is dedicated to the blessed memory of **Late Inspector Garba Usman**, fondly called **Baba Auwalu**, the founder of Hossana Goodnews Fellowship, **Bompai Police Barracks, Kano**. He raised the banner of righteousness high in the Nigerian Police Force and gave his all for the gospel of the kingdom of our Lord Jesus Christ winning many. And to all the apostles of the Lord Jesus Christ whose primary place of kingdom assignment is within the gamut of the marketplace of nations – victory is sure!

Thus says the Lord, your Redeemer, the Holy One of Israel: I am the Lord your God, Who teaches you to profit, Who leads you in the way that you should go. (Isaiah 48:17, AMP)

1

DEAR APOSTLE IN THE MARKETPLACE

THE BASIC DEFINITIONS

An apostle is a messenger. A messenger operates between two parties – the sender and the receiver. They take 'the message' from the sender to the receiver. So the parties involved in this relationship are immediately evident as follows:

i. The Sender
The sender is God.

ii. The Message
The message is Christ crucified, His kingdom and His righteousness.

iii. The Messenger
The messenger is the believer who has wilfully chosen to permanently defer to God and be sent by Him however He pleases, and no matter the cost.

iv. The Receiver

Any person, people or people system yet to accept *The Message*.

The Marketplace

The marketplace is a platform (mostly parachurch in structure and essence) where there is bargain; buying and selling, profit and loss. The marketplace is a networking hub that constantly connects buyers to sellers. Some of the notable features of the marketplace include commerce and enterprise.

An Apostle in the Marketplace

Therefore, an apostle in the marketplace is a believer who has unconditionally chosen to defer to God, specifically sent to preach Christ crucified, His kingdom and His righteousness within the marketplace. These functionaries bring to bear the witness of Christ in word and deed within their assigned portion of the marketplace.

MY TESTIMONY

In the beginning

I have been privileged by God to be a part of the greatest cause on earth: the kingdom of God and His righteousness. He has sovereignly and graciously ordered the trajectory of my life in the service orbit of the kingdom of His dear Son. His grace has been sufficient every step of the way. His mercy has helped me stay the course, not swerving to the left or right. His love and faithfulness

> An apostle in the marketplace is a believer who has unconditionally chosen to defer to God, specifically sent to preach Christ crucified, His kingdom and His righteousness within the marketplace

have formed the cornerstone of my faith and filled my heart with gravitas for His business.

At the age of seven, I gave my life to Christ; I had my first significant encounter at the age of thirteen and got commissioned to start a global apostolic network called the Remnant Christian Network at twenty-five. Like Paul, I am most grateful not to have been disobedient to the heavenly vision. My service lane in the kingdom was paved by my obedience to divine instructions that absolutely made no sense. The strides I made came from things that could have be described as absurd. I grew through numerous opportunities given to me to serve. I served as an usher, and later taught Bible study classes for new believers at my local assembly. The measure of God's grace for each stage was awesome.

In the process of time, in my late teenage years, I became 'stagnant' in my Christian life. It was almost like my Christian experience had plateaued. This lingered until it became a serious source of concern. So I decided to shut down everything else and devote myself entirely to seeking the Lord in prayer and fasting. The Lord responded in a rather direct and cryptic message to me thus:

'I have called you to be an apostle.'

I did not know who an apostle was; neither did I have the

faintest clue to what the apostolic ministry entailed. So I ran to my pastor and asked him to explain to me who an apostle was. My pastor, utterly oblivious of my dealings with the Lord, laughed hysterically. In his humanity, he told me not to consider myself as one. My pastor at the time was a good man but seemed not to have the capacity to handle what the Lord was doing with me. I knew I heard God, but my pastor's answer plunged my teenage mind many degrees into the depth of confusion.

> I realised I had climbed to the peak of my Christian experience at the time and needed to descend and start a fresh ascent to a new peak on the mountain of God

The ray of light from the throneroom of heaven that hit the tablet of my heart to reveal God's eternal counsel for my destiny was potent, yet frail. So, I decided to take one of the greatest risks of my Christian faith – lean wholly into what God said to me despite my pastor's dismissive counsel. When I did, I realised I had climbed to the peak of my Christian experience at the time and needed to descend and start a fresh ascent to a new peak on the mountain of God. This would open up a mighty portal for experiencing higher and deeper measures of God's grace. And the rest, they say, is history.

More than a quarter-century later, I would boldly say, by the mercies of God, God was right! Needful to add, I was ushered into a concatenation of encounters that would build in me the robust facility of apostleship in keeping with God's purpose for my life.

THE APOSTOLIC MANDATE

I started like every other believer who loved the Lord and wanted their life to count for something eternal. The grace of God upon my life gave me great access into Scriptures – I taught the Bible with sublime ease and great grace. I maximised every opportunity I had to serve the Lord.

Shortly after my university education and national service, the Lord appeared to me and gave me the mandate that would spawn what is now known as the Remnant Christian Network.

I knew I had been called into the fivefold ministry – as an apostle with the primary assignment of striving for the rebirth of apostolic Christianity. But the route to the fullness of my apostleship would lead me into another kind of apostleship. This kind required my full attention, participation and service in the *marketplace* as much as in the *fivefold*.

It was obvious that I was on another peak on the Lord's mountain and needed to descend and make a fresh ascent to yet another peak. The Lord was yet again breaking my wineskin at the seams. The usual route to ministry, especially in the fivefold, was 'full-time.' But among other things the Lord instructed in the mandate, He clearly said to me:

'I will give you a job, you shall invest in many destinies, and a great network shall be born.'

The mandate above definitely brought my lofty theology to dust. The norm then was to abandon all 'secular work' and face ministry *full-time*. In an inverse reality, here was the Lord telling me He would give me a job – an opportunity to serve in the marketplace while fully serving in the fivefold! To be honest with you, it was overwhelming.

I did not quite understand it, but just like the Lord spoke to me about calling me to be an apostle years earlier, there was no sliver of doubt in my heart that He was calling me to ascend higher in kingdom service. Each time the Lord has asked me to climb higher in kingdom service; I notice that the experiences of the previous height were not sufficient to sustain me. I would feel like a toddler again, thus making me need Him even more. The higher, the needier!

> **The route to the fullness of my apostleship would lead me into another kind of apostleship. This kind required my full attention, participation and service in the marketplace as much as in the fivefold.**

This is the way of the kingdom – maturity is measured by how much we are willing to permanently defer to God and have Him lead us as He would. Jesus said,

I assure you, most solemnly I tell you, when you were young you girded yourself [put on your own belt or girdle] and you walked about wherever you pleased to go. But when you grow old you will stretch out your hands, and someone else will put a girdle around you and carry you where you do not wish to go. (John 21:18, AMP)

This is the core of the apostolic – totally submitting to God for Him to send you wherever He will. This is very important because it forms the substructure upon which the entirety of kingdom service is founded.

A STRANGE KIND OF APOSTLESHIP

About one year after the Lord gave me the mandate for my ministry, the job He had promised came in the most miraculous way possible as a sign to let me know it was time to ascend higher in kingdom service. Before that, I was a classroom teacher. My new job would pay me many times more than my previous classroom teaching job. I was no longer confused as to why it came – the apostolic mandate. And for the next sixteen years, the Lord would have me build an intensive apostolic ministry both within the body of Christ and in the marketplace (traversing the wild gamut of Nigeria's oil and gas industry).

> The core of the apostolic - totally submitting to God for Him to send you wherever He will.

People would wonder nonstop at how I was able to joggle being an apostle to the body of Christ and in the marketplace; and how I was able to get gracious results in ministry within the body of Christ and the marketplace. Well, I would never cease to tell them that God's grace is always released to ensure excellent performance with respect to God's mandate, relative to the measures in Christ that He allots to His sons and daughters.

God commands it; He releases all requisite resources to make it good. So it has had nothing to do with me really but everything to do with God and His unfailing ability to finish whatever He starts and execute what He commands through any yielded vessel. I am privileged to be a recipient of His grace and apostleship within the body of Christ.

Being an apostle to the body of Christ, I have tonnes of experiences and encounters to share, but that's a matter altogether for another discourse.

My apostleship in the marketplace has had to run concurrently with my apostleship within the body of Christ. The Great King of Heaven commanded it so, and He gave all the increase. I completely understand it is a sharp deviation from the status quo of kingdom service.

Being an apostle in the marketplace requires the same rigours of training, discipline and intensity as being an apostle within the body of Christ. It requires God's wisdom and power, divine equipping, equipment, and resources to extend the frontiers of God's kingdom throughout the layers and curves of the marketplace. It entails unleashing God's authority and power within the multifarious corridors of the marketplace.

Thankfully, some examples can be drawn from the riches of Scripture to grasp this peculiar kind of apostleship. We shall discuss these throughout this discourse.

EMPHASIS ON THE MARKETPLACE

I defined the marketplace earlier as a platform (mostly parachurch in structure and essence) where there is bargain: buying and selling, profit and loss. The marketplace is a networking hub that constantly connects buyers to sellers. There is always buying and selling – of goods, services, souls, etc in the marketplace. It is characterised by commerce and enterprise, which always yield gold (material resources). There is bargain which always results to profit and loss. The marketplace of the nations is concisely captured in the following passage of Scripture:

> *And earth's businessmen...Their merchandise is of gold, silver, precious stones, and pearls; of fine linen, purple, silk, and scarlet [stuffs]; all kinds of scented wood, all sorts of articles of ivory, all varieties of objects of costly woods, bronze, iron, and marble. Of cinnamon, spices, incense, ointment and perfume, and frankincense, of wine and olive oil, fine flour and wheat; of cattle and sheep, horses and conveyances; and of slaves (the bodies) and souls of men!* (Revelation 18:11-13, AMP)

The above passage roughly captures the significant sectors of industry. The opening words, 'And earth's businessmen', do full justice to the product catalogue and the ilk of those who populate the marketplace of the nations. Note that the most expensive merchandise in the marketplace of nations is not gold and such other material things but the souls of men! The souls of men are what heaven and hell are after. The most sophisticated form of trading and commerce is the one that involves the souls of men. Jesus said,

> **For what will it profit a man if he gains the whole world, and loses his own soul?** (Mark 8:36, NKJV)

Note that there is profit and loss (of souls) in the marketplace of the nations of the world.

I would like to build a context for the marketplace, which shall serve as the boundary for this discourse. The marketplace is any platform a believer is sent to by God to serve as an ambassador of the kingdom of heaven. It is parachurch because it does not directly relate to the church. That is, its operations are completely constituted outside the 'four walls' of the church. In my book GO INTO ALL THE WORLD, I asserted that the fivefold ministry and their supporting ministries, which are usually carried out within the church, constitute ten per cent of kingdom service, while ninety per cent of kingdom service happens outside the church. This is because the kingdom is bigger than the church. The kingdom is vast and expansive and stretches far beyond the borders of the church. The church is limited in structure and constitution because it is strictly comprised of those who have eternal life by believing in Jesus. While the kingdom is comprised of anywhere the lordship and kingship of Christ are established. (This I have sufficiently addressed in the two volumes of my book KINGDOM RECALIBRATION).

> Note that the most expensive merchandise in the marketplace of nations is not gold and such other material things but the souls of men! The souls of men are what heaven and hell are after.

The burden of this epistle is to surgically reach out to all who have a call within the marketplace. For this discourse, I would like to categorise the callings in the marketplace into the following:

1. PRIMARY

Comprises believers whose major kingdom assignment is in the marketplace or includes the marketplace. This includes believers who are elite technocrats and professionals operating in the corporate world: large scale, medium scale and small-scale business-people, athletes, entertainers and people working in entertainment. High, medium and low government functionaries, media people, artisans, educationists, hairstylists, fashion entrepreneurs, social media influencers etc. are also in this category. These believers rise to the pinnacle of service and influence in the marketplace. The scope of their assignment may or may not include active kingdom service within the church.

2. SECONDARY

This comprises believers whose major kingdom assignment is within the church but have to have a shallow, sporadic interface with the marketplace. Their involvement with the marketplace is strictly on a part-time basis and is usually meant to get gold in order to do God's work. These are believers who are heavily involved with kingdom service within the church but have to engage the marketplace on the side for material resources. These believers typically do not rise to the pinnacle of service and influence in the marketplace.

3. TRANSIENT

This comprises believers whose primary kingdom assignment is within the church or in the marketplace but are required to serve in the church or in the marketplace for a season. Depending on what the instruction from God is, they may or may not rise to the very pinnacle of service and influence in the marketplace. But the impact of their work in the marketplace is visible and seminal.

> The burden of this epistle is to surgically reach out to all who have a call within the marketplace.

4. NULL

This comprises believers whose major kingdom assignment has zero interface or intersection with the marketplace. Their kingdom service is strictly confined to the four walls of the church.

EXHORTATIONS FOR THE APOSTLE IN THE MARKETPLACE

If you are convinced by God that your kingdom assignment has something to do with the marketplace, congratulations. But after the congratulations, you should know you have been entrusted with the noblest and most solemn task on earth.

You see, the Almighty God, Zion's undisputed Monarch, Most Excellent of the Excellencies, whose throne is surrounded by thunder blasts and lightning that defy the expressive capacity of language, before whom ageless sages and vassal monarchs cast their crowns depends on you! Yes, you!

As powerful as God is, He will not invade the marketplace

- your portion of the marketplace without your cooperation and partnership. God's investment in you is meant to empower you to make the most of all opportunities in your space within the marketplace for kingdom profit. And, no, opportunity does not only come once; it comes each time you interlock your faith with God's will. The processes, dealings, training, anointing, prayers, and fasting are to prepare you for the field. Oh yes, the field. It is time to take it to the field. The Lord Himself has declared that,

> *I tell you, raise your eyes and observe the fields and see how they are already white for harvesting.* (John 4:35, AMP)

> **As powerful as God is, He will not invade the marketplace - your portion of the marketplace without your cooperation and partnership.**

It is a great time to be alive and be in the employ of Heaven's Great King. The fields of the marketplace are ripe for harvesting. All you need to do is to arise in obedience and put the sickle in!

Below are some noteworthy exhortations for the apostle in the marketplace:

- Being sent by the Lord into the marketplace is a result of the election of grace, not human genius.
- To remain relevant as God's apostle in the marketplace, you must always be ready and willing to take new instructions from Him. Without instruction, whatever you are doing would be vulnerable to satanic disruption and destruction.

- The instructions of God are loaded with the technology for appropriating the dimensions of God. In faithfully executing God's instructions, you erect structures that can trap and make the most of His dimensions within your portion of the marketplace. God's dimensions can be trapped on earth, in the marketplace, when His apostles build according to the measurements, blueprints and schematics of heaven.

- The dominion of God in heaven can be replicated in every square inch of the marketplace through priesthood.

- Intensive consecration and extensive intercession must be in place at all times. These would help generate the requisite defence against the onslaught of dark forces that seek to control the marketplace. The popular belief that marketplace apostles are exempted from the rigours of priesthood is a corpulent lie of the devil.

- Ensure you make it top priority to explore God nonstop like an astronaut explores space; through prayer and the ministry of the word. This is because the operational strategies that are needed can only be revealed by God. The apostle must learn to discover their God-given tools and how to use them proficiently. Once they find out how the tools work, it becomes theirs! The moment they are revealed to you, they become yours. When they become yours, you become a person of stature.

- A person of stature can, through direct interface with God, change and override the laws that govern the marketplace. This is why even when the odds are not serendipitously stacked for you and your natural resources are shut down, you can access a realm in God with resources that are limitless and cannot be hijacked by even the most vicious hounds of hell. And then, you can use the wisdom acquired to dominate your portion of the marketplace.

- God would continue to deal with you like a potter beats clay so that you can have enough capacity to host His wisdom and power and enough capability to deploy them accurately.

- Diligently guard your heart, for in it are boundaries of life. God measures how far a man can go by looking at the boundaries of his heart. A person whose heart is enlarged through the discipline of the Holy Spirit would be given the capacity of a thousand people.

- It is not about numbers with God but about capacity. God would rather give one yielded person the capacity of one thousand people than give one thousand people the ability of one man.

- God only backs what He inspires. He is not human, so His utterances are sometimes made in direct opposition to our humanity. Whatever is not sourced from Him cannot be supported with His wisdom and power. This is why every project that is not congruous with the pattern in heaven will be filled by another spirit that is surely not God's.

- Note that under God and with God, you can only win by righteousness - even in the marketplace!

2

THE MARKETPLACE OF NATIONS

THE DIFFERENCE BETWEEN THE EARTH AND THE WORLD

To fully understand the marketplace of nations, we must first fully grasp the essential difference between the earth and the world. Then we would study the world and its systems as they directly affect the nations (which host the marketplaces) within it.

> **THE EARTH** *is the Lord's, and the fullness of it,* **THE WORLD** *and they who dwell in it*
> (Psalm 24:1, AMP, emphasis mine)

The Hebrew word for **earth** in the verse of Scripture above is **erets,** and, it means the physical, geographical planet earth with all its resources. It is simply land and water.

The Hebrew word for **world** is **tebel,** which roughly translates to an organised group of people living in a defined geographical space. It is taken from the words **yabal,** which means to bring forth, lead as in a procession, cause to flow; and ***yebuwl***, which means to produce (that is a crop), which figuratively means wealth. The root word for ***tebel*** is associated with the word ***Tubal*** (whose full name is Tubal-Cain, an offspring of Cain [Genesis 4:22]). We shall talk more about Tubal-Cain shortly.

Jesus, in describing the believers, said,

You are the salt of the EARTH... (Matthew 5:13, NKJV, emphasis mine)

You are the light of the WORLD... (Matthews 5:14, NKJV, emphasis mine)

The word earth in the Scripture above in Greek is ghay, and it means solid ground, the vast expanse of land on which humankind lives. The word world in the Greek is kosmos and it practically means an orderly arrangement, a decoration. Just as the earth physically hosts humankind, so does the world socially and systematically host humankind's order.

> To fully understand the marketplace of nations, we must first fully grasp the essential difference between the earth and the world.

The concept of the sharp difference between the earth and the world is the same through both Testaments. While the earth is mainly the physical ground space of the planet, the world is the orderly arrangement and decoration that powers all people systems. The earth and the world are the Lord's. We shall focus more on the world in this discourse because it bears God's heartbeat – people!

Using computing parlance, we could easily describe the earth as the *hardware* while the world is the *software* that is housed by and runs in the earth – and runs the earth. The earth is, therefore, the container while the world is the content. So in one simple sentence: the earth is GEOGRAPHY while the world is PEOPLE.

JESUS SENT US INTO 'THE WORLD' AND NOT 'THE EARTH'

In sending His disciples, Jesus commanded them to

"Go into all the world ..." (Mark 16:15, NKJV)

This is a simple technicality, but it would provide a very robust framework for our entire discourse.

Note, Jesus said *world*, not *earth*! Note also, the word ALL in the command strategically covers the entire gamut of the world. This forms the basis of what we refer to as the Great Commission.

So, it is simple: Jesus sent (sends) His disciples to PEOPLE, not to GEOGRAPHY!

I have extensively covered this in my book entitled GO INTO ALL THE WORLD.

THE WILD ADVENTURES OF CAIN AND THE BIRTH OF THE WORLD SYSTEM

The Murder

The story of Cain is a total tragedy. When we read the story, we are almost tempted to think that perhaps the judgement meted to him by God was a little too harsh and perhaps he could have been spared the extreme darkness that became his legacy. But no, Cain had every opportunity to make things right yet chose to embrace darkness. We shall consider this shortly.

The most crucial moment in Cain's life is captured in the following verse of Scripture:

> *So the Lord said to Cain, "Why are you angry? And why has your countenance fallen? If you do well, will you not be accepted? And if you do not do well, SIN LIES AT THE DOOR. AND ITS DESIRE IS FOR YOU, BUT YOU SHOULD RULE OVER IT."* (Genesis 4:6-7, NKJV, emphasis mine)

This was immediately after Cain got miffed because God respected his brother Abel over him and accepted his brother's offerings but rejected his. Yet the reason is simple -Abel was respected by God, and his offerings were accepted; not out of partiality (which is a trait inconsistent with God's eternal righteousness and justice) on God's part. Abel sincerely honoured God, so it was only normal for him to have thought of God as deserving of the very best of the work of his hands. He, therefore, went out of his way to select the best of his livestock and offer to God. The quality of Cain's offering revealed how much honour he had for God - which was low, by the way! God would not have it. After all, the earth and its fullness all belong to Him. So God would neither

> **Cain had every opportunity to make things right yet chose to embrace darkness.**

respect Cain nor accept his offering (Genesis 4:1-5).

Now Cain was not only unhappy with God's response toward him and his offering, but he also began to nurse murderous thoughts toward his brother. There was someone else in the picture – someone whose slovenly whispers Cain lent his heart to – the same crooked character that lurked in the shadows and deceived his parents – the devil!

Note that God did not mince words when He told Cain in clear terms that sin lay at the door and would waste no time in possessing him at the slightest chance it gets. God would rather that Cain rule over it. So let's consider this for a moment. Sin originated with Lucifer-turned-the devil. The Bible speaks of Lucifer thus:

> *You were perfect in your ways from the day you were created, till iniquity was found IN you* (Ezekiel 28:15, NKJV, emphasis mine)

Note that iniquity was found IN and not ON him. It means he brazenly pitched against God's will by an act of His will and decided to become a vector (carrier, host and distributor of sin). Sin originated with the devil in heaven (1 John 3:8). The iniquity the devil carried (and still carries) was (and still is) communicable and would invade any space given to it.

So, when God said *'...sin lies at the door'*, He meant that the devil (being the custodian and dispenser of sin), had set a booby trap for Cain's soul. He did this by being wickedly nimble and ready to pounce on, invade, pillage and rule over Cain's soul like an army of viruses – the moment Cain opened the door of his heart! It was a red alert warning of sorts from God, but Cain ignored it. Of course, the devil's stratagem was not brute force but seemingly benign suggestions and subterfuge. He would tirelessly keep knocking and serenading on the door of Cain's heart till Cain opened and let him in (Psalm 10:9). And what better tool for the devil to use to work on Cain than his animosity and envy toward his brother! Cain opened up the door of his heart to the devil, and, voila, the devil wasted no time in filling his soul with

> The devil is incapable of having a relationship with man; he can only transact. Every deal he has with man, be it active or passive, is a skewed business transaction.

darkness. The sin which dangerously lay at the door had become a first-class guest in Cain's heart. So when he slew his brother, Abel, Cain defiantly rejected God's love by refusing to love his brother and flagrantly established a partnership with the devil to upend God's order on earth. Scripture reveals that the reason Cain slew his brother was that he belonged to the devil! (1 John 3:10-12).

In no time, the devil's work in Cain's soul became obvious. The hatred and envy that Cain felt toward his brother Abel had mutated into thoughts of murder. The murderous thoughts rotted further into a murder plot. The murder plot deteriorated into an act of murder; which finally gave the devil total ownership of Cain's soul as the transaction was now complete. Unwittingly but wilfully, Cain sold his soul to the devil for the temporary high of settling some score with his brother. He murdered his brother. Indeed, every space given to the devil is a transaction. The devil is a master trader. The Bible speaks of him thus:

By the abundance of your TRADING
You became filled with violence within,
And you sinned;
Therefore I cast you as a profane thing
Out of the mountain of God;
And I destroyed you, O covering cherub,
From the midst of the fiery stones
(Ezekiel 28:16, NKJV, emphasis mine)

The devil is incapable of having a relationship with man; he can only transact. Every deal he has with man, be it active or passive, is a skewed business transaction. His transactions are not guided by righteousness. For him, anything goes, and the end justifies the means. This is why I always say that the maxim *the end justifies the means* is not a principle of God – it originates from the devil! No one trades with the devil and emerges a net winner! The devil's transactions always produce violence that leads to banishment from the 'mountains of God'.

The devil is like termite on wood and fire on dry hay – he is incapable of construction. This is why he lays waste whatever space is given to him. He tears to pieces whatever soul is connected to him. The Psalmist brilliantly captures this thus:

O Lord my God, in thee do I put my trust: save me from all them that persecute me, and deliver me: Lest HE TEAR MY SOUL LIKE A LION, RENDING IT IN PIECES, while there is none to deliver. O Lord my God, if I have done this; if there be INIQUITY IN MY HANDS (Psalm 7:1-3, KJV, emphasis mine)

The devil's rulership over Cain's soul was established when Cain dipped his hands in iniquity, and the devil tore his soul to pieces!

For the record, the devil is not to be talked to, consorted with or related with, but ruthlessly resisted. Jesus Christ, God's pattern man, successfully resisted the devil at the beginning of His earthly ministry (Matthew 4: 1-11) and when He was about to fulfil the most critical part of His earthly assignment by going to the cross (Matthew 16:23). Of course, for one to successfully resist the devil, they must first fully submit themselves to God (James 4:7)!

The Consequences

After Cain murdered his brother, the heft of consequences came rushing like an avalanche. With Cain's parents, the devil's transaction earned him costly disobedience. With Cain, the devil raised his operational bar higher and achieved murder (blood)! You might ask why Cain's offence received harsher punishment than that of his parents. Here is why: Cain's parents (Adam and Eve) were commanded by God not to eat of the tree of the knowledge of good and evil with the consequence of violation clearly spelt out as death. The devil deceived them, and they went ahead to eat of the tree of the knowledge of good and evil and died (spiritually).

Cain, on the other hand, was not explicitly warned by God not to kill his brother. But God clearly warned him about the consequence of treading the path of animosity and envy toward his brother – total possession by sin. I have explained that when God said, 'Sin lies at the door', He was by extension referring to the devil having the poise and wicked intent of an opportunistic predator. And should Cain let him in, the devil would invade, pillage and takeover his soul.

While Cain's parents' punishment was a total disconnection from God, Cain's punishment was a total connection to the devil. Cain's parents' spirits were disconnected from God (thus leading to spiritual death) – theirs was termination. Cain's soul was connected to the devil (thus leading to endless exploration of the sinful realm, with the devil as tour guide) – his was a dark progression.

In response, God cursed the ground for the sakes of Cain's parents relative to their disobedience thus:

> **And to Adam He said, Because you have listened and given heed to the voice of your wife and have eaten of the tree of which I commanded you, saying, You shall not eat of it, THE GROUND IS UNDER A CURSE because of you; in sorrow and toil shall you eat [of the fruits] of it all the days of your life.** (Genesis 3:17, AMP, emphasis mine)

Cain was cursed thus:

> **And [the Lord] said, What have you done? The voice of your brother's blood is crying to Me from the ground. And now YOU ARE CURSED BY REASON OF THE EARTH, WHICH HAS**

OPENED ITS MOUTH TO RECEIVE YOUR BROTHER'S [SHED] BLOOD FROM YOUR HAND. When you till the ground, it shall no longer yield to you its strength; you shall be a fugitive and a vagabond on the earth [in perpetual exile, a degraded outcast]. (Genesis 4:10-12, AMP)

With the murder of Abel, Cain became the first man to spill blood on earth! He would also be the first man to be cursed. He wilfully sowed his brother's blood into the earth and reaped a bitter curse. Abel's blood cried to God from the earth's murky amplification chambers for vengeance (Hebrews 12:24). The mechanism by which Abel's blood joined forces with the earth to slam a curse on Cain is a matter altogether reserved for another discourse. But justice was served, and a multipronged curse descended on Cain.

Among the things Cain was cursed with is the fact that he would be a fugitive, vagabond, perpetual exile and degraded outcast – unsettled for the rest of his life! It means there would be no rhythm to his life – his existence would be filled with endless chaos. This sadly, is very characteristic of the devil, who the Bible describes as follows:

- He Roams Like A Marauding Beast
Be well balanced (temperate, sober of mind), be vigilant and cautious at all times; for that enemy of yours, THE DEVIL, ROAMS around like a lion roaring [in fierce hunger], seeking someone to seize upon and devour. (1 Peter 5:8, AMP, emphasis)

- Prince of the power of the air

And you He made alive, who were dead in trespasses and sins, in which you once walked according to the course of this world, according to the PRINCE OF THE POWER OF THE AIR, the spirit who now works in the sons of disobedience (Ephesians 2:1-2, NKJV)

The designation *'Prince of the power of the air'* means the devil has neither an established throne nor a firm operational base. He floats and wanders nonstop across the vast terrain of the cosmos. He is a cosmic nomad that is incapable of settling anywhere. He is unstable and incapable of brooking any form of order.

God, on the other hand, shines steadily like a lighthouse and harbours or supports no form of undulation. He is forever stable. This is why He is forever dependable (James 1:17)

- He is a restless spirit

> When the UNCLEAN SPIRIT is gone out of a man, he walketh through dry places, SEEKING REST, AND FINDETH NONE.
> (Matthew 12:43, KJV, emphasis mine)

The character and nature of the unclean spirit is that it is essentially eternally restless – this is so true of the devil and his minions. From the moment the devil and all his cohorts were cast out of heaven, they have not had one-googolth fraction of a second's rest. They are sentenced to experiencing an eternity of sanity-splitting seizures. In him and them, are millennia of unresolved, pent-up restlessness. Restlessness is a curse that alights on any angelic creature that is disconnected from God by an act of their will. The devil and his cohorts are like tensed strings that are pulled and would not rest easy for all eternity. They would forever vibrate – they will forever be unable to keep still and enjoy God's eternal peace.

God, on the other hand, rests and gets refreshed (Genesis 2:2; Exodus 31:17). And it is because He rests that He can give rest to those who serve Him (Matthew 11:28; Hebrews 4:9-11).

So, effectively, through Cain, the devil could express himself unrestrained on earth. The devil would pioneer the things he had in mind for which he was cast out and given no space in heaven.

A CIVILISATION APART FROM GOD

> Then Cain went out from the presence of the Lord and dwelt in the land of Nod on the east of Eden. And Cain knew his wife, and she conceived and bore Enoch. And he built a city, and called the name of the city after the name of his son — Enoch. To Enoch was born Irad; and Irad begot Mehujael, and Mehujael begot Methushael, and Methushael begot Lamech. Then Lamech took for himself two wives: the name of one was Adah, and the name of the second was Zillah. And Adah bore Jabal. He was the father of those who dwell in tents and have livestock. His brother's name was Jubal.

He was the father of all those who play the harp and flute. And as for Zillah, she also bore Tubal-Cain, an instructor of every craftsman in bronze and iron. And the sister of Tubal-Cain was Naamah. (Genesis 4:16-22, NKJV)

Cain left the eternal stability and rest that are endemic to God's presence and dwelt in the land of Nod – Nod means wandering! I have written a bit about Cain in my book entitled Kingdom Recalibration. I will write more about him here as it relates to the kernel of this discourse. Cain left the presence of God and dwelt in a certain land called Nod. Now the *presence of God* means *the face of God*, which by extension is where His focus, consciousness and infinite attention span (which sum up to His government) are. To be in God's presence means to be in God's face – to be under His direct supervision, care, tutelage and nurture. Of course, this requires total, wilful reverence and deference to Him. In His presence is eternal stability and rest.

Cain was effectively deactivated from God's radar. The moment he did that, he was completely on his own – unhedged and ready to be fully utilised by the devil. He left eternal stability for mundane instability. There, his mind became the hub for antigod technologies and concepts. He began to receive dark paradigms. He built a city – he founded a civilisation that was completely independent of God – entirely underpinned by satanic architecture and engineering.

Cain built systems that entrenched independence from God and accelerated the deterioration of the fall. The devil was in every detail and in every inch of the dark progression – supplying all the corrupt energy and resources to establish systemic rebellion against God on earth. This would serve as the foundation for what would be known as the world system, which has driven human civilisation for millennia and gives impetus to the New World Order. The devil is the prince of the power of the air. He rules through sin and reigns through iniquity. His goal was to establish the kingdom of darkness on earth that would militate against the kingdom of God for all. He found a worthy, willing partner and subject in Cain. Cain was, therefore, the first apostle of the kingdom of darkness on earth.

> Cain built systems that entrenched independence from God and accelerated the deterioration of the fall. The devil was in every detail and in every inch of the dark progression - supplying all the corrupt energy and resources to establish systemic rebellion against God on earth.

He became the prototype of the antichrist on earth. We can see the dark wisdom at work through the policies he implemented. The cardinal principle by which Cain ran everything was direct independence from God. The nature, character and orientation of the civilisation that Cain built did not have God in view. It was a monolith of human-centred godlessness. What Cain was saying was simple; he was loudly and defiantly declaring, 'God, I can do without you. I can build without you, and I can live without you – without your policies, principles and presence.' What he built drew no modicum of inspiration whatsoever from God's system in Eden.

Cain's legacy of darkness was carried on by his children as follows:

1. Polygamy

Lamech, a fifth- generation descendant of Cain, decided to push the frontiers of unrighteousness by marrying two women at once. This, of course, was an aberration and distortion of God's original order and design of one man and one woman within the context of matrimony. Lamech's life was indeed an evolution of darkness.

> The cardinal principle by which Cain ran everything was direct independence from God. The nature, character and orientation of the civilisation that Cain built did not have God in view. It was a monolith of human-centred godlessness.

2. Tent making and livestock farming

Jabal, one of the sons of Lamech, invented tent making and livestock farming. Tent making was one of the earliest forms of real estate. Livestock farming was practically the commercialisation of that which was not originally meant to have a price tag; thereby creating man-made employment. Man-made employment would now be a further distortion of the original design and order of God. Man-made employment would make man depend on his fellow man for livelihood. When God originally created man, he gave him employment by commanding him to manage and defend the Garden of Eden (Genesis 2:15). This was in keeping with the original design and order for man to be wholly dependent on God. Jabal's *job creation initiative*, as beneficial as it seemed, was a total deviation from the original order and design of dependence on God.

Jabal's system of employment ensures the necessity of looking up to God for assignment and purpose is completely obliterated. It is humanistic at its core – it ensures that man looks up to man instead of God in matters of destiny, assignment and purpose. This operation of darkness is at the foundation of the marketplace today. Today's marketplace is designed to ensure employment takes the place of God in people's lives. People wake up very early, hardly fellowshipping with God, rush out to resume their places of work early, come back home late and barely have time for anything else. This happens all week. For those fortunate enough to have weekends to themselves, the weekends are hardly enough for anything other than preparing for the following week. This is true for both the 'self- employed' and those who are working at paid employments. The system deifies jobs and commonises God.

3. Music

Jubal, also one of the sons of Lamech, invented the craft of making musical instruments and the art of playing them. This would lay the foundation for music-powered entertainment. Music-powered entertainment is at the heart of popular culture, which is one of the products of the world system today.

Music and musical instruments were neither created by man nor the devil. They were created by God! And everything that God created was primarily designed to exist for His good pleasure, including music (Revelation 4:11). So music and musical instruments did not originate from earth but originated from heaven. Music goes on in heaven for all eternity with the accompaniment of musical instruments (Revelation 5:8-9). Music-powered entertainment again takes away the focus from God to man. It is also a distortion of the original purpose of music – to give God pleasure.

With the help of the one who was once a resident of heaven (the devil), Jubal created a system that would be a corrupt imitation of heaven's order for the further corruption of humankind. Music-powered entertainment aims to quiet the piece of eternity in everyone's heart that connects them to God. It is a systemic distraction from the gaping void occasioned by the absence of God from the heart of the average unbeliever. The external rhythm, melodies, harmonies and instrumentation are designed to drown and mute the voice of God that reaches forth to everyone's heart from eternity's vast expanse.

4. Metallurgy – tools and weapons of war

Tubal-Cain, also one of Lamech's sons invented metallurgy and the craft of converting metals to different tools and weapons. Mining metals from the ground and forging tools and weapons from them required great skill. This would go on to form the core of human defence system.

Again, man's security and protection was meant to come from God, but in the civilisation founded by Cain, man chose not to trust in the Lord for safety and security but in the works of his hands. So, men would rather trust in forged metals to bring them deliverance than the unmatchable protection of Jehovah!

A man who is not secure in God exudes overwhelming foulness. Insecurity is the foundation for war games, witchcraft, manipulations, espionage, and every foul-spirit-aided human arrangement that breeds distrust, deception and lies.

> **The civilisation Cain pioneered was self-based, a system that would keep people perpetually apart from God.**

The common denominator of all the systems outlined above is self - self -propagation (Lamech), self-support (Jabal), self - entertainment (Jubal) and self-defence (Tubal-Cain). The civilisation Cain pioneered was self-based, a system that would keep people perpetually apart from God.

MESOPOTAMIA: THE CRADLE OF CIVILISATION

Mesopotamia is generally referred to as the cradle, beginning and origin of human civilisation on earth. It is the birth place of the systematisation of all human activities. The word Mesopotamia means *between two rivers*. This is because the land mass that forms Mesopotamia is situated between the Tigris-Euphrates river system. The Tigris-Euphrates river system is formed by the rivers Tigris and Euphrates, which happen to be two out of the four river heads that went out of Eden (Genesis 2:10-14).

As we shall soon see, Mesopotamia is very crucial to understanding the origin, composition and outlay of the earth, the world and all the systems that drive it. This is because it is not only the origin of the natural human civilisation, but also the birth place of the patriarch of faith, Abraham (Acts 7:2), whom God used to pioneer the civilisation of faith, culminating in the birth of Jesus, who would birth the new creation (Matthew 1:1-16).

A careful study of the meaning of the two rivers that power Mesopotamia reveals something very stunning thus:

Tigris means spear, arrow-like, fast, and arrowhead.

Euphrates means to gush forth, break forth, and have a breakthrough.

It is worthy of note that Tigris and Euphrates jibe clearly in meaning with Tubal-Cain, whom we have studied earlier, and established that he invented the craft of forging metals into tools and weapons of war. His work established, built out and shaped the human defence system. He did not only invent. He taught others to do the same, which earned the designation of *the instructor of every craftsman in bronze and iron*. The meaning of his name is as follows:

Tubal means to cause to flow, to bring forth, to produce.

Cain means spear.

Now, what is the implication of all this? It is simple:

Euphrates and **Tubal** figuratively mean wealth and, by extension, **Economy.**

Tigris and Cain connote **Government.**

Remember that in the beginning, man's God-designed, primary assignment in the Garden of Eden was thus:

> *Then the Lord God took the man and put him in the Garden of Eden to TEND and KEEP it.*
> (Genesis 2:15, NKJV, emphasis added)

The word **tend** in Hebrew is **abad**, and it means to cultivate, cause to flourish, manage. This is economy.

The word **keep** in Hebrew is **shamar**, and it means to hedge about (as with thorns) for defence: to protect. This is government.

MESOPOTAMIA: THE CRADLE OF CIVILISATION

A nation is generally understood to mean a group of people that share a common ancestry, language, interest, value, culture, and geographical space. Scripture, however, further throws light on the concept of a nation to mean people systems (I have touched on this briefly in my book **Go Into All The World**). This means the concept of nations is broadened and deepened to include anywhere (tangible or intangible) people converge around a common goal, identity, interest etc. So nations could be on-ground or off-ground. As long as there is a system that houses a specific group of people with common interests, we can say there is a nation. There are millions of nations on earth today! An aggregation of all the people systems makes up the world system.

Nations (whether on-ground or off-ground, virtual or geographical) are defined by two main pillars: ECONOMY and GOVERNMENT. The economy is emblemised and embodied by the currency, while government is emblemised and embodied by a flag. This is why every sovereign, geographical nation on earth is represented by its currency and flag.

ECONOMY and GOVERNMENT, therefore, form the twin platforms or cornerstones of the marketplace. So, the millions of nations (people systems) are underpinned by the economy and government. Every apostle of God in the marketplace will operate in either or both of these two systems. Economy and government transcend money and flags. They represent something far more systemic, expansive, extensive and tentacular. Economy and government are woven into every inch of the world system. Every living soul on earth today is directly affected by economy and government. This is what the marketplace of nations is about.

> The concept of nations is broadened and deepened to include anywhere (tangible or intangible) people converge around a common goal, identity, interest etc.

JESUS CHRIST THE SON OF DAVID, THE SON OF ABRAHAM (MATTHEW 1:1)

Scripture reveals the two genealogies of our Lord Jesus Christ thus:

1. *The natural genealogy that traces back to Adam (Luke 3:22-38)*

Jesus Christ's natural genealogy was meant to strategically position Him as the last Adam - the first and only one to be born and die sinless after the order of the first Adam to create the possibility for the new creation - with a brand new life (1 Corinthians 15:45). As the last Adam, He successfully closed the book of the old humanity and opened a new one through His death, burial and resurrection so that anyone who would be reborn after Him would be a brand new, unprecedented creature with no prehistory or antecedents (2 Corinthians 5:17).

2. *Spiritual genealogy that traces back to David and Abraham (Matthew 1:1)*

Jesus Christ is traced to David because of the throne (Government). And He is traced to Abraham because of the covenant. Abraham's modus operandi was economic because he managed an enormous household in which he raised 318 men (Genesis 14:14) and wielded a lot of material wealth (Genesis 13:2). His life practically had the full dimensions of an economy – wealth and administration. The word *economy* is coined from the Greek word *oikonomia* meaning household management. Abraham's walk, work and legacy of faith are forever established by the redemptive work of Jesus. Abraham's patriarchy (Romans 4:11) is directly drawn from God's patriarchy – God, who is the Father of all (Ephesians 4:6).

> **ECONOMY and GOVERNMENT, therefore, form the twin platforms or cornerstones of the marketplace.**

God is both Father (who runs the divine economy [Ephesians 1:10; 3:2; Colossians 1:25]) and King (who runs an eternal government [Psalm 45:6]). He embodies and manifests these through the office of The Christ (Colossians 1:19). Anyone who is in Christ is engrafted into the economy and government of God. Therefore, they would need to deliberately and consistently engage God in fellowship and submission to enjoy His economy and align to His government. This is why God's household – the church, is populated by kings and priests (Revelation 5:10). God's nation is a royal priesthood (1 Peter 2:9).

In Christ, we exercise dominion and gain access to the vastness of God's authority by submitting to Him. Like the twenty-four elders in heaven who reign with God by continuously falling before Him, worshipping Him and casting down their crowns before His throne (subsuming their authority in His authority) [Revelation 4:10]. To truly worship God, one has to first accept that God is greater than them! So each time a believer submits to God, they align themselves to - His government's indestructible dominion structures. They can wield His matchless authority in their space of the marketplace. God's economy is aligned to and enjoyed through priesthood; which is characterised by prayer. Through effective priesthood, a believer unlocks and lays hold of the resources of heaven that are trapped in, and administered through God's economy. God's government is based on His eternal authority and His economy on the fullness of grace embodied and administered by Christ!

> In Christ, we exercise dominion and gain access to the vastness of God's authority by submitting to Him. Like the twenty-four elders in heaven who reign with God by continuously falling before Him.

Christ is the sole Administrator of God's economy. It is through Christ that God's grace-based resources flow to every member of His house. Christ also is the King who runs the eternal government of heaven on earth so that it would be on earth as it is in heaven. Economy and government therefore, do not originate from man on earth but from God in heaven.

The economic and governmental dimensions of God's operation within the believer are meant to thoroughly furnish them for every good work in the marketplace. These dimensions can only be operated by the wisdom and power of God, which again, are fully embodied by Christ (1 Corinthians 1: 24).

PHILIP AND THE ETHIOPIAN EUNUCH: THE APOSTOLIC MEETS ECONOMY AND GOVERNMENT

Now an angel of the Lord spoke to Philip, saying, "Arise and go toward the south along the road which goes down from Jerusalem to Gaza." This is desert. So he arose and went. And behold, a man of Ethiopia, A EUNUCH OF GREAT AUTHORITY UNDER CANDACE THE QUEEN OF THE ETHIOPIANS, WHO HAD CHARGE OF ALL HER TREASURY, and had come to Jerusalem to worship, was returning. And sitting in his chariot, he was reading Isaiah the prophet. Then the Spirit said to Philip, "Go near and overtake this chariot."

So Philip ran to him, and heard him reading the prophet Isaiah, and said, "Do you understand what you are reading?" And he said, "How can I, unless someone guides me?" And he asked Philip to come up and sit with him. The place in the Scripture which he read was this:

*"He was led as a sheep to the slaughter;
And as a lamb before its shearer is silent,
So He opened not His mouth.
In His humiliation His justice was taken away,
And who will declare His generation?
For His life is taken from the earth."*

So the eunuch answered Philip and said, "I ask you, of whom does the prophet say this, of himself or of some other man?" Then Philip opened his mouth, and beginning at this Scripture, preached Jesus to him. Now as they went down the road, they came to some water. And the eunuch said, "See, here is water. What hinders me from being baptized?"

Then Philip said, "If you believe with all your heart, you may."

And he answered and said, "I believe that Jesus Christ is the Son of God."

So he commanded the chariot to stand still. And both Philip and the eunuch went down into the water, and he baptized him. Now when they came up out of the water, the Spirit of the Lord caught Philip away, so that the eunuch saw him no more; and he went on his way rejoicing.

(Acts 8:26-39, NKJV, emphasis added)

This passage tidily captures God sending His apostle (Philip) to go to a specific address (a portion of the marketplace) to preach Christ to the Ethiopian Eunuch who embodied the government and economy of Ethiopia by his service under Candace, the queen of the Ethiopians at the time.

The Ethiopian eunuch was a high ranking *government* official in charge of the entire treasury (*economy*) of Ethiopia. In His infinite wisdom, God orchestrated that Philip reach out to him with the gospel of the Lord Jesus Christ by strategically positioning himself and overtaking the eunuch's chariot. The Holy Ghost who supernaturally handled Philip's commute seemed to be in a hurry to save the Ethiopian eunuch. The eunuch had to be divinely overtaken by Philip for him to have an encounter with the gospel. It was clear the eunuch's case was that of a special rescue mission –incongruous with quotidian outreach protocol but fully sponsored by God's sovereignty. The whole operation was commanded and carried out with a great sense of urgency.

The Ethiopian eunuch was preached to, received the gospel, got saved and was baptised in one moment's stretch. After which, Philip was caught up by the Holy Ghost and taken to another place for another assignment. The Ethiopian eunuch would never see Philip again, but what he received from the Lord through Philip's ministry changed his life forever. The Bible does not follow up on the Ethiopian eunuch's work after his encounter with Philip. But imagine what a man with such means and influence would do for the kingdom of our Lord Jesus Christ in Ethiopia. To date,

Ethiopia remains one of the oldest repositories for documents germane to the Christian faith and thought; suggesting how much God wants the marketplace of nations overtaken and conquered with the message of the gospel of the Lord Jesus Christ.

In these last days, there is no doubt the Lord has placed a particular emphasis on the apostolic takeover of the marketplace of the nations. The Lord is ready to commit enormous resources to support the victorious emergence of the apostolic horde whose unique mission is the marketplace of nations; from coast to coast, street to palace, right across all walks of life and in every people system, present and future! It is time to arise, take formation under the Lord's command and descend on the harvest of the marketplace of the nations in the name of the Lord! Victory has already been won by our Lord, who saw Satan fall like lightning to eternal inglorious depths (Luke 10:18).

> **In these last days, there is no doubt the Lord has placed a particular emphasis on the apostolic takeover of the marketplace of the nations.**

3

BABYLON AND EGYPT: THE TWIN PLATFORMS OF THE MARKETPLACE

The burden against Tyre.
Wail, you ships of Tarshish!
For it is laid waste,
So that there is no house, no harbor;
From the land of Cyprus it is revealed to them.

Be still, you inhabitants of the coastland,
You merchants of Sidon,
Whom those who cross the sea have filled.
And on great waters the grain of Shihor,
The harvest of the River, is her revenue;
And she is a MARKETPLACE FOR THE NATIONS.

Be ashamed, O Sidon;
For the sea has spoken,
The strength of the sea, saying,
"I do not labor, nor bring forth children;
Neither do I rear young men,

Nor bring up virgins."
When the report reaches EGYPT,
They also will be in agony at the report of Tyre.
Cross over to Tarshish;

Wail, you inhabitants of the coastland!
Is this your joyous city,
Whose antiquity is from ancient days,
Whose feet carried her far off to dwell?
Who has taken this counsel against Tyre, the crowning city,

Whose merchants are princes,
Whose traders are the honorable of the earth?
The Lord of hosts has purposed it,
To bring to dishonor the pride of all glory,
To bring into contempt all the honorable of the earth.

Overflow through your land like the River,
O daughter of Tarshish;
There is no more strength.
He stretched out His hand over the sea,
He shook the kingdoms;
The Lord has given a commandment against Canaan

To destroy its strongholds.
And He said, "You will rejoice no more,
Behold, THE LAND OF THE CHALDEANS,
This people which was not;
Assyria founded it for wild beasts of the desert.

BABYLON AND EGYPT: THE TWIN PLATFORMS OF THE MARKETPLACE

They set up its towers,
They raised up its palaces,
And brought it to ruin.

(Isaiah 23:1-13, NKJV, emphasis added)

This prophetic piece of poetry powerfully captures the flurry of activities that take place in the marketplace of the nations. Human interplay as expressed through endless travels, trade, coordination of commerce and the huge transcultural shifts are some of the things highlighted in the passage above.

In order for us to fully grasp the biblical concept of the marketplace of nations, we would need to study Egypt and Babylon. As we shall see, Egypt and Babylon both came out of Mesopotamia, and they both connote economy and government.

> All people systems under heaven are broadly categorised into economy (as typified by Egypt) and government (as typified by Babylon)

The passage above connects the *land of the Chaldeans* (which is Babylon) to Egypt through an elaborate marketplace system that sufficiently captures enterprise and industry and everything else in-between under heaven. And as we shall soon see, Egypt and Babylon are the two all-encompassing, metaphoric platforms that comprehensively capture all activities within the marketplace of the nations.

So God's apostles, whose primary area of assignment is the marketplace of the nations, would either serve in a sector, sphere and people system that is directly or tangentially -

immediately or remotely – connected to *economy* or *government*.

Economy broadly covers commerce, trade, merchandise, and any arrangement that supports the exchange of goods and services for some value. The fulcrum of economy is profit and prosperity. Economy is driven by buying and selling. So if your portion of the marketplace is primarily driven by buying and selling, it means you are on the economic platform of the marketplace.

Government broadly covers any arrangement that supports the formulation, administration and enforcement of laws, codes, rules, regulations within a people system. The fulcrum of government is order. Government is driven by authority and power. So if your portion of the marketplace is primarily driven by the exercise of authority and the use of power, it means you are on the governmental platform of the marketplace.

For emphasis' sake, all people systems under heaven are broadly categorised into economy (as typified by Egypt) and government (as typified by Babylon). If you stretch any people system well enough and decompose it to its basic operation, you would find out it belongs to either the economic or governmental platform of the marketplace of the nations.

Note that, as far as the nations (people systems) are concerned, God is the Ultimate Governor. The Bible says,

For the kingdom is the Lord's: and He is the GOVERNOR *among the nations* (Psalm 22:28,

KJV, emphasis added)

As far as economy is concerned, God is the Possessor of heaven and earth and lacks nothing (Genesis 14:19, 22).

BABYLON

The word *Babylon* is the word *Babilim* from the native Babylonian tongue, and it means *gate of the gods*. Gates in Scriptures connote authority (Psalm 24:7; Matthew 16:18). That it is the gate of the gods (not God Almighty), means it is a portal – a command tower for spirits – a place where spirits can exercise dominion. Thus it is a place open for the superimposition of extraterrestrial civilisations of unrighteous provenance upon the realms of men. This is where spirit beings grant men access to extraterrestrial resources for building antigod systems – a place where men by diabolic affiliations give up their will in service of dark, vagabond, and restless forces totally subservient to the devil. It is the place where the arrow-head of human government, which gives direction and perspective to human civilisation is whetted. The following verse of Scripture captures this horrendous reality of Babylon being a gate of the gods:

> *Babylon the great has become a dwelling place of demons, a prison for every foul spirit, and a cage for every unclean and hated bird!* (Revelation 18:2-3, NKJV)

The church is the only place God can call home on earth. This is why it is called the household of faith (Galatians 6:10). Jacob revealed that the house of God is the gate of heaven – a portal through which heaven maintains constant engagement with earth (Genesis 28:17). Paul revealed that the church (God's household) is a conduit through which the unbeatable wisdom of God is made known to the dark cosmic forces (Ephesians 3:10). It is the command tower where the Spirit of the Most High God exercises maximum dominion for the total conquest of the world's component systems (Revelation 11:15).

Because Babylon is a gate of the gods, there are usually heavenly gatekeepers – extraterrestrial beings stationed at the fulcrums and epicentres of systems, which coordinate legislations, decrees, edicts and proceedings within those systems. It was one of those gate keepers called the Prince of Persia that barricaded the parcel sent from the third heaven to Daniel on account of his intercessory demands. The Prince of Persia successfully intercepted Daniel's heavenly package by resisting God's messenger for twenty-one days (Daniel 10:1-14). The Prince of Persia could successfully interfere with Daniel's divine correspondence because Daniel's spiritual milieu was 'under' his keep.

THE ORIGINS OF BABYLON

After the incorrigible hedonism that peaked in the days of Noah, God would no longer put up with the corruption in the world, which was defiantly powered by man's iniquity. God moved to do something that would seem like a brutal mechanical reset of creation to restore sanity on earth. The flood came and wiped off humankind. Noah's family, consisting of Noah and his wife; his three sons and their wives – eight souls in total were charged by God to exit the ark and repopulate the earth (Genesis 8:15-17). The fate (so to speak) of humanity hung on these eight people (just as it hung on Adam and Eve in the beginning).

Upon the cessation of the flood and the exit of Noah and his family and all the animals with them from the ark, God restated the mandate He gave to Adam and Eve in the beginning; established the groundwork for what would flower into the age of human government and made a covenant to never cut off mankind with flood forever (Genesis 9: 1-17).

Noah's three sons – Shem, Ham and Japheth took on the task of repopulating the earth (Genesis 9:18-19) and immediately began to reproduce after the flood (Genesis 10:1).

In keeping with the establishment of human government, people began to be grouped according to their languages, lands, families and nations (Genesis 10:5).

A STRANGE TWIST

Immediately after the flood, Noah became a farmer, planted a vineyard and began to fill himself up with wine. Perhaps that was his way of coping with the post-traumatic stress of the flood that weighed heavily on his sanity. To have gone through all he did and be saddled with the onerous task of ensuring that humankind did not go extinct was indeed burdensome. He however, turned to the wrong place (the product of his vineyard) to get some solace. One day he got so filled with wine that he lost himself and became naked in his tent. Ham, his second son, erroneously looked upon his father's nakedness and reported to his two brothers, who would not join in looking upon their father's nakedness. When Noah regained himself and learned what his son, Ham, had done, he pronounced a curse on his seed and blessed his brothers (Genesis 9:20-27).

Note that Noah did not curse Ham directly; he pronounced a curse on one of Ham's sons – Canaan – instead (Genesis 9:25) while he blessed Shem and Japheth directly (Genesis 9:26-27).

The impact of Noah's curse on Ham's seed would have far-reaching consequences. It opened up Ham's family to the pillaging forces of darkness. And not long afterwards, someone who would rise in iniquity and catch the mantle and spirit of Cain would be born through one of his seeds. Below is Ham's genealogy:

> *The sons of Ham were Cush, Mizraim, Put, and Canaan. The sons of Cush were Seba, Havilah, Sabtah, Raamah, and Sabtechah; and the sons of Raamah were Sheba and Dedan.* **CUSH BEGOT NIMROD; HE BEGAN TO BE A MIGHTY ONE ON THE EARTH. HE WAS A MIGHTY HUNTER BEFORE THE LORD; THEREFORE IT IS SAID, "LIKE NIMROD THE MIGHTY HUNTER BEFORE THE LORD." AND THE BEGINNING OF HIS KINGDOM WAS BABEL,** *Erech, Accad, and Calneh, in the land of Shinar. From that land he*

BABYLON AND EGYPT: THE TWIN PLATFORMS OF THE MARKETPLACE

went to Assyria and built Nineveh, Rehoboth Ir, Calah, and Resen between Nineveh and Calah (that is the principal city). Mizraim begot Ludim, Anamim, Lehabim, Naphtuhim, Pathrusim, and Casluhim (from whom came the Philistines and Caphtorim). Canaan begot Sidon his firstborn, and Heth; the Jebusite, the Amorite, and the Girgashite; the Hivite, the Arkite, and the Sinite; the Arvadite, the Zemarite, and the Hamathite. Afterward the families of the Canaanites were dispersed. And the border of the Canaanites was from Sidon as you go toward Gerar, as far as Gaza; then as you go toward Sodom, Gomorrah, Admah, and Zeboiim, as far as Lasha. These were the sons of Ham, according to their families, according to their languages, in their lands and in their nations. (Genesis 10:6-20, NKJV, emphasis added)

Ham's genealogy is an eclectic ensemble of some of the most villainous characters, nations and peoples in Scriptures! But considering them one after the other is beyond the purview of this present discourse.

Our person of interest is Nimrod, who happens to be the one who harnessed the potential of the age of human government to build the first kingdom on earth. He reopened the portal that Cain opened by building an entire civilisation apart from God in his day. This portal of iniquity that supported absolute independence from God was closed on account of the earth-wide annihilation of humankind by the flood. The flood only wiped out human beings. It did not mete out the same punishment to the evil spirits that lurked on the earth. All it took for Cain's portal to be reactivated was for Ham to commit a very costly blunder that bordered on violation of authority as it had to do with despising his father.

Nimrod cultivated, grew and maximised influence throughout the earth. By building a kingdom, he was able to leverage on his well-harnessed clout to institutionalise the iniquitous legacy of Cain, which came to a head when men attempted to build the tower of Babel. The seed of unrighteousness that Ham planted was unwittingly multiplied into a forest of godlessness in the days of Nimrod.

THE CHARACTER, STRUCTURE, NATURE AND OPERATIONAL PARADIGM OF BABYLON

Babylon is set up to be run by government and governance. All its glory, splendour and powers are designed to be maximised by governmental systems, institutions and paradigms. The book of Daniel detailedly captures the structure and operational paradigms of Babylon.

The first time Babel [Babylon] appears in Scripture, it is revealed as a kingdom – a governmental system (Genesis 10:10). We have already established that Babylon means the gate of the gods – a domain where extraterrestrial beings are given the right of way to exert dominion. The governmental system by which Babylon was run was therefore underpinned by the wisdom of spirits.

In the days in which the governmental system that was

BABYLON AND EGYPT: THE TWIN PLATFORMS OF THE MARKETPLACE

> Babylon is set up to be run by government and governance. All its glory, splendour and powers are designed to be maximised by governmental systems, institutions and paradigms.

founded by Nimrod would achieve maturation and global dominance, Nebuchadnezzar was king. There was thorough coordination, order and organisation of near-perfect, Brobdingnagian proportions. With this sophisticated system in place, Nebuchadnezzar's rule would transcend the great shores of Babylon to the four corners of the known world of the time. His rule and reign made him a suzerain monarch of sorts. He was called the king of kings (Daniel 2:27). The robust governmental infrastructure under his command made it easy for him to make Babylon a superpower, thereby pioneering what we now know as globalisation. Nebuchadnezzar made Babylon the world's melting pot by putting together the most excellent technocratic system of antiquity consisting of the finest assemblage of the brightest minds from different nations. There was a very rigorous recruiting system perfected to distil only the best into the service of the realm of Babylon. The Bible says,

> *'Youths without blemish, well-favored in appearance and skillful in all wisdom, discernment, and understanding, apt in learning knowledge, competent to stand and serve in the king's palace — and to teach them the literature and language of the Chaldeans. And the king assigned for them a daily portion of his own rich and dainty food and of the wine which he drank. They were to be so educated and so nourished for*

three years that at the end of that time they might stand before the king' (Daniel 1:4-5, AMP)

This pristine ensemble of the best and brightest youths scooped from different nations was to be groomed into the best 'think tank' of antiquity. They were to formulate the very best policies that would maintain Babylon's hallowed place and space as *the tip of the spear of human civilisation*. Their wisdom would be the fuel that would power the Babylonian governmental machine, which consisted of:

> *...the satraps, the deputies, the governors, the judges and chief stargazers, the treasurers, the counselors, the sheriffs and lawyers, and all the chief officials of the provinces* (Daniel 3:2, AMP)

Of course, being the gate of the gods, stature (of whatever kind) in Babylon was spirit-driven. Magicians, soothsayers, the Chaldeans (a people whose primary occupation was witchcraft and astrology) prospered immensely in Babylon. Babylon was not only the world's cultural melting pot; it was also a spiritual melting pot of the nations. The negative and the positive supernatural were given a platform to find full expression. This was why Daniel and his Hebrew comrades were lumped up with the practitioners of dark arts to form the *elite wisdom army* of Babylon through an extremely rigorous recruitment process to

> There was a very rigorous recruiting system perfected to distil only the best into the service of the realm of Babylon.

which they were all subjected to.

Daniel and his Hebrew comrades, who had been conscripted into Nebuchadnezzar's wisdom army from Israel, stood out because the Spirit of the Most High God was upon them. According to the testimony of Nebuchadnezzar, the 'spirit of the holy gods' dwelt in Daniel, whom he nicknamed Belteshazzar. The same Spirit that aided Daniel in solving a conundrum that defied the wisdom of all the practitioners of dark arts in Babylon. This was why Nebuchadnezzar called Daniel the 'master of magicians' (Daniel 4: 8-9). It did not matter what spirit was involved in Babylon; all that mattered was results! Anyone who delivered lofty results gained ascendancy in the governmental ladders of Babylon.

To be an effective functionary in those sombre days of Babylonian global dominance, one had to learn the science, technology, art and craft of government and governance. One had to acquire the elite training of technocrats. And, most importantly, one had to be fully dedicated to a being of extraterrestrial provenance – a spirit, which could imbue them with the wisdom and power to consistently deliver eyebrow-raising results. Daniel and his Hebrew comrades had to be fully dedicated to the Holy One of Israel to be effective representatives of the Most High God in Babylon. Their lifestyle, conduct and persuasions were shaped by their devotion to the Most Holy One! Their environment did not dictate their convictions. The convoluted order in the realm of Babylon did not breach their resolve to ensure God's pleasure remained their number one priority. So, when it came down to it, and they had to choose between pleasing Babylon at the expense of pleasing God Most High, they threw all caution to the wind and stuck to pleasing God. Not minding the deleterious consequences their resolve would expose them to.

So, from Daniel 1:4-5, which we have quoted overleaf, the following characteristics of Babylon could be deduced:
- Babylon has a keen eye for potential
- Babylon does not forcefully oppose; it persuasively co-opts
- Babylon does not kill; it overwhelms
- Babylon seeks to use all that one is and has
- Babylon does not endow but can make the most of endowments
- Babylon harvests the best to build its systems and retain its territorial integrity

The recruitment academy into the civil service of Babylon was a balanced mix of the major pillars of philosophy. The curriculum is a congealed by-product of the best distillates from the best schools of thought. This academy was administered by an ascetic – a master of eunuchs, (a clique of public servants who have permanently sacrificed sexual pleasure for 'kingdom' service therefore, having no care in the world except to ensure Babylon gains supreme ascendancy in the comity of nations). The primary duty of the ascetic was to get the best students into this academy. The curriculum was designed to last

They progressively maintained their consecration to God, and in no time, they brought the whole of Babylon to its knees!

for three years, during which each student was:

- To be treated to a daily provision of the king's meat (eat the choicest cuisines – concocted through the culinary perfection at the king's table). The king's meat represents doctrine (Matthew 6:11, 4:4)
- Drink the best wines which were exclusively available to the king. Wine represents the Spirit (Ephesians 5:18; Acts 2:15-17)
- To acquire a new Babylonian name befitting of the quality of their work in Babylon. A name represents stature and ranking (Genesis 12:2; Philippians 2:9-10)

Daniel and his Hebrew comrades rejected the king's food and wine but were given Babylonian names (whose meanings were mostly tied to the service of Babylonian deities). Below are their Babylonian names and their meanings:

- Daniel was given the Babylonian name Belteshazzar which means 'Bel *protect the life of the king*'. Bel was the head of the Babylonian pantheon – the chief god of the gods of Babylon.
- Hananiah was given the Babylonian name Shadrach which means '*Command of* **Aku**'. Aku was the Babylonian god of the moon.
- Mishael was given the Babylonian name Meshach which means '*Who is as* Aku'.

Azariah was given the Babylonian name Abed-nego which means '*Servant/slave of* **Nebo**'. Nebo was the Babylonian god of wisdom.

So why would Daniel and his comrades accept something that

seemed to have an overt alliance with other gods as their Babylonian names and reject something as seemingly benign and useful as royal food and wine? This was because the food and wine were capable of defiling them (destroying the infrastructure of their consecration to God), while the names were like certificates that had the capacity to open administrative doors for them through the governmental structures and corridors of power in Babylon. While the food and wine could mess them up internally, the names were external tools they could use to draw attention to their God. Consequently, they became ten times better than their peers. They progressively maintained their consecration to God, and in no time, brought Babylon to its knees!

EGYPT

Egypt roughly means black land (named possibly after its very rich dark humus soil which is enlivened by the Nile River for maximally productive agricultural activities). The Aramaic and Hebrew word for Egypt is Mizraim which means mound or fortress. Mizraim is one of the sons of Ham, as we have already considered earlier in this chapter. A superficial consideration of the meaning of the name Mizraim would make it look almost the same as Babylon. But as we shall soon see, though Egypt built up a formidable defence system with one of the best military of antiquity, its outstanding might was mainly economic. This is why Egyptian civilisation developed along the Nile River largely because the river's annual flooding ensured reliable, rich soil for growing crops. The Nile would become synonymous with Egypt's agricultural production and economic resources, which increased from generation to generation.

Abraham, the father of faith, and his descendants would once and again go to Egypt to seek economic sustenance in times of drought. At one point in history, Egypt built an economy so strong that it was the only nation that survived a seven-year global economic collapse that brought countless nations to their knees and brought them in their numbers within its borders seeking economic help.

Egypt precociously shored up and strategically built its economy with so much abundance and tact that it became recession-proof. When the global economic tsunami hit, it did not as much as experience mild tremors. This was Egypt in the days of God's servant, Joseph. So, for our discourse, we shall focus on Egypt as a supreme economic force among nations. I therefore, we shall briefly consider Egypt in the days of Joseph.

> Egypt precociously shored up and strategically built its economy with so much abundance and tact that it became recession-proof. When the global economic tsunami hit, it did not as much as experience mild tremors.

Joseph was seventeen years of age when he got admitted into the training academy of destiny within the shores of Egypt. The training would last thirteen long years. He had to endure protracted unpleasantness, betrayal, abandonment, imprisonments, and much more in the mixed bag of his grating curriculum. Upon graduation, he would stand before Pharaoh, the supreme leader of Egypt and a potentate across the then known world.

In the days of Joseph, Egypt was arguably the world's superpower. So Pharaoh was not only the ruler of Egypt; he was indeed a ruler recognised in the known world of that time. Pharaoh would be shaken by a dream that no magician in the whole of Egypt could interpret. Joseph's graduation would coincide with the most crucial and urgent royal dilemma in Egypt. Pharaoh's trouble happened to be something that only Joseph had been well-trained and equipped to solve. Joseph's interpretation of Pharaoh's dream would reveal that Egypt and indeed, the rest of the world were on an economic precipice – there was imminent financial Armageddon on the horizon of the world. And whether or not Egypt and the rest of the world would survive depended heavily on how the nation handled the situation. This would all unravel in the next fourteen years.

> In the days of Joseph, Egypt functioned as one giant economic machine. Joseph was its driver!

So within Egypt's borders lay economic solutions to the world's problems and the protagonist in the centre of it all was Joseph, while his God championed it all. In an instant, Joseph outshone the horde of magicians, influence peddlers and political heavyweights in Egypt to become both Pharaoh's number one adviser and Egypt's overseer. His thirteen-year travails in the grating academy of destiny would prepare him for eighty years of glory! He held and steered Egypt's heartbeat – its economy, for more than two generations.

In the days of Joseph, Egypt functioned as one giant economic machine. Joseph was its driver! (Genesis chapter 37 through chapter 41)

THE MAJOR DIFFERENCE BETWEEN EGYPT AND BABYLON IS IN PHARAOH'S AND NEBUCHADNEZZAR'S DREAMS

Pharaoh's Dream, Its Interpretation by Joseph and Its Fulfilment

Then it came to pass, at the end of two full years, that Pharaoh had a dream; and behold, he stood by the river. Suddenly there came up out of the river seven cows, fine looking and fat; and they fed in the meadow. Then behold, seven other cows came up after them out of the river, ugly and gaunt, and stood by the other cows on the bank of the river. And the ugly and gaunt cows ate up the seven fine looking and fat cows. So Pharaoh awoke. He slept and dreamed a second time; and suddenly seven heads of grain came up on one stalk, plump and good. Then behold, seven thin heads, blighted by the east wind, sprang up after them. And the seven thin heads devoured the seven plump and full heads. So Pharaoh awoke, and indeed, it was a dream. Now it came to pass in the morning that his spirit was troubled, and he sent and called for all the magicians of Egypt and all its wise men. And Pharaoh told them his dreams, but there was no one who could interpret them for Pharaoh.

Then Joseph said to Pharaoh, "The dreams of Pharaoh are one; God has shown Pharaoh what He is about to do: The seven good cows are seven years, and the seven good heads are seven years; the dreams are one. And the seven thin and ugly cows which came up after them are seven years, and the seven empty heads blighted by the east wind are seven years of famine. *This is the thing which I have spoken to Pharaoh. God has shown Pharaoh what He is about to do. Indeed seven years of great plenty will come throughout all the land of Egypt; but after them seven years of famine will arise, and all the plenty will be forgotten in the land of Egypt; and the famine will deplete the land. So the plenty will not be known in the land because of the famine following, for it will be very severe. And the dream was repeated to Pharaoh twice because the thing is established by God, and God will shortly bring it to pass.*

"Now therefore, let Pharaoh select a discerning and wise man, and set him over the land of Egypt. Let Pharaoh do this, and let him appoint officers over the land, to collect one-fifth of the produce of the land of Egypt in the seven plentiful years. And let them gather all the food of those good years that are coming, and store up grain under the authority of Pharaoh, and let them keep food in the cities. Then that food shall be as a reserve for the land for the seven years of famine which shall be in the land of Egypt, that the land may not perish during the famine." So the advice was good in the eyes of Pharaoh and in the eyes of all his servants. And Pharaoh said to his servants, *"Can we find such a one as this, a man in whom is the Spirit of God?"*

Now in the seven plentiful years the ground brought forth abundantly. So he gathered up all the food of the seven years which were in the land of Egypt, and laid up the food in the cities; he laid up in every city the food of the fields which surrounded them. Joseph gathered very much grain, as the *sand of the sea, until he stopped counting, for it was immeasurable. And to Joseph were born two sons before the years of famine came, whom Asenath, the daughter of Poti-Pherah priest of On, bore to him. Joseph called the name of the firstborn Manasseh: "For God has made me forget all my toil and all my father's house." And the name of the second he called Ephraim: "For God has caused me to be fruitful in the land of my affliction." Then the seven years of plenty which were in the land of Egypt ended, and the seven years of famine began to come, as Joseph had said. The famine was in all lands, but in all the land of Egypt there was bread. So when all the land of Egypt was famished, the people cried to Pharaoh for bread. Then Pharaoh said to all the Egyptians, "Go to Joseph; whatever he says to you, do." The famine was over all the face of the earth, and Joseph opened all the storehouses and sold to the Egyptians. And the famine became severe in the land of Egypt. So all countries came to Joseph in Egypt to buy grain, because the famine was severe in all lands.* (Genesis 41: 1-8; 25-38; 47-57, NKJV)

I have quoted copiously from the Bible here, nearly all the relevant verses on Pharaoh's conjoined dreams, its interpretation by Joseph, and its fulfilment. So that there would be no shade of doubt about how essentially economic it was in theme and construct. The key elements of the dream were livestock and crops – food, an everlasting need of man under heaven. Anything that would happen to the system (agriculture) by which this basic need of man (food) is produced could lead to an extinction-level event for humanity. It posed an existential threat to the human race.

What was more interesting was that the problem was global in scope. A sure famine was coming like a category five hurricane - built to sweep across all nations of the world. The plague was as certain sunrise and sunset. Nothing could be done to stop it, but something could be done to manage it and profit from it. One man seemed to have all the answers. Joseph!

It would please the Lord to strategically groom and showcase Joseph to Pharaoh, Egypt's supreme ruler, just before the most significant fourteen years of his reign. The solution to the global famine foreseen by Pharaoh was exclusively placed in Joseph's hands. This would present an economic opportunity for Egypt and lead to the rise of Joseph throughout the realm of Egypt.

> A sure famine was coming like a category five hurricane - built to sweep across all nations of the world. The plague was as certain sunrise and sunset. Nothing could be done to stop it, but something could be done to manage it and profit from it. One man seemed to have all the answers. Joseph!

Nebuchadnezzar's Dream and Daniel's Interpretation

"You, O king, were watching; and behold, a great image! This great image, whose splendor was excellent, stood before you; and its form was awesome. This image's head was of fine gold, its chest and arms of silver, its belly and

BABYLON AND EGYPT: THE TWIN PLATFORMS OF THE MARKETPLACE

thighs of bronze, its legs of iron, its feet partly of iron and partly of clay. You watched while a stone was cut out without hands, which struck the image on its feet of iron and clay, and broke them in pieces. Then the iron, the clay, the bronze, the silver, and the gold were crushed together, and became like chaff from the summer threshing floors; the wind carried them away so that no trace of them was found. And the stone that struck the image became a great mountain and filled the whole earth.

"This is the dream. Now we will tell the interpretation of it before the king. You, O king, are a king of kings. For the God of heaven has given you a kingdom, power, strength, and glory; and wherever the children of men dwell, or the beasts of the field and the birds of the heaven, He has given them into your hand, and has made you ruler over them all – you are this head of gold. But after you shall arise another kingdom inferior to yours; then another, a third kingdom of bronze, which shall rule over all the earth. And the fourth kingdom shall be as strong as iron, inasmuch as iron breaks in pieces and shatters everything; and like iron that crushes, that kingdom will break in pieces and crush all the others. Whereas you saw the feet and toes, partly of potter's clay and partly of iron, the kingdom shall be divided; yet the strength of the iron shall be in it, just as you saw the iron mixed with ceramic clay. And as the toes of the feet were partly of iron and partly of clay, so the kingdom shall be partly strong and partly fragile. As you saw iron mixed with ceramic clay, they will

> mingle with the seed of men; but they will not adhere to one another, just as iron does not mix with clay. And in the days of these kings the God of heaven will set up a kingdom which shall never be destroyed; and the kingdom shall not be left to other people; it shall break in pieces and consume all these kingdoms, and it shall stand forever. Inasmuch as you saw that the stone was cut out of the mountain without hands, and that it broke in pieces the iron, the bronze, the clay, the silver, and the gold – the great God has made known to the king what will come to pass after this. The dream is certain, and its interpretation is sure."

(Daniel 2:31-45, NKJV)

It is unmistakably clear from the passage above that the content of Nebuchadnezzar's dream was purely governmental. The theme, motif and interpretation of the dream all point to kingdoms and conquests. I have written briefly about the different kingdoms spoken of in the dream in the second volume of my book **Kingdom Recalibration**. The dream itself is an avant-garde motion picture of the governmental constructs, curves and manoeuvres of the human civilisation beginning from the days of Nebuchadnezzar down through centuries of cyclical conquests and defeats among suzerain and vassal kings and kingdoms. The ultimate conquest of which shall be established by the kingdom of God!

You see, Nebuchadnezzar was given a cryptic visual of what would transpire in human history through centuries that would lead right up to the worldwide conquest of the kingdoms of the world by the kingdom of our God and of His Christ.

Nebuchadnezzar's royal mind did not have the requisite capacity to fathom this dream, neither did any practitioner of the dark arts in Babylon. This would set the stage for the manifestation of Daniel, who concluded his interpretation by saying, *'The dream is certain and the interpretation is sure.'* This means no force either in nature, in the quarters of hell or the realm of men can stop it from coming to pass.

APOSTLES AFTER THE ORDERS OF JOSEPH AND DANIEL

Both Joseph and Daniel came to national prominence by interpreting the dreams of kings. The dreams could not be construed by the most sophisticated and advanced practitioners of dark arts in the kingdoms in which they lived. The interpretations they gave came straight from God. They were made to oversee the affairs of the territory as a result of the supernatural wisdom that was at work in them, which was occasioned by the Spirit of God.

The presence of God in Joseph's life made him prosperous - imbued him with the rare messianic and economic wisdom with which he oversaw the world's largest economy and helped failing nations from collapsing under the austere weight of hunger. Joseph commanded and commandeered prosperity wherever he served - from Potiphar's house to the throneroom of Egypt. Joseph was made an overseer of Egypt, his primary focus being Egypt's economy (Genesis 39:2; 41:37-39).

The hand of God on Daniel's life configured him into a towering government expert beyond compare. As such, he became the number one government consultant and adviser in Babylon.

> *Then King Nebuchadnezzar fell on his face, prostrate before Daniel, and commanded that they should present an offering and incense to him. The king answered Daniel, and said, "Truly your God is the God of gods, the Lord of kings, and a revealer of secrets, since you could reveal this secret." Then the king promoted Daniel and gave him many great gifts; and he made him ruler over the whole province of Babylon, and chief administrator over all the wise men of Babylon.* (Daniel 2:46-49, NKJV)

Joseph's dream, ordeals, sojourn and triumph in Egypt were totally orchestrated by God. At his lowest, most melancholic moments – completely estranged from the much-needed warmth, comfort and support of family – shafted

> **The hand of God on Daniel's life configured him into a towering government expert beyond compare. As such, he became the number one government consultant and adviser in Babylon.**

and billowed by the jealousy and treachery of his brethren, God Himself shepherded Joseph (Psalm 80:1). In Genesis 45:7, Joseph testified thus,

BABYLON AND EGYPT: THE TWIN PLATFORMS OF THE MARKETPLACE

And GOD SENT ME before you to preserve a posterity for you in the earth, and to save your lives by a great deliverance. (Genesis 45:7, NKJV, emphasis added)

In the verse of Scripture above, Joseph summarises his life as one giant apostolic odyssey- with God sending him ahead of his brothers to Egypt to preserve a posterity and orchestrate a great deliverance for them. Note that Joseph said *God sent him* ahead – He was an apostle of God in Egypt's marketplace. He lived with a sent mentality in Egypt. He knew he was on an errand in Egypt. His loyalty was first to God in all things!

> Joseph's dream, ordeals, sojourn and triumph in Egypt were totally orchestrated by God. At his lowest, most melancholic moments - completely estranged from the much-needed warmth, comfort and support of family - shafted and billowed by the jealousy and treachery of his brethren, God Himself shepherded Joseph

In Daniel 9:2, Daniel begins to pray for the deliverance of his people, having understood by books that they were only meant to spend seventy years in Babylon. So, all the ordeals, travails, trials and tribulations were the training and transportation systems that God arranged to equip and send Joseph and Daniel forth to Egypt and Babylon. When God sends forth a person, He arranges circumstantial training and transportation to reinforce them with righteousness and get them to the destination of their assignment. This is to both test and strengthen their character while they serve in the exact place where God wills.

Therefore, God sends apostles to the marketplace to preserve remnants and extend His salvation among the nations; and not primarily for fortune, fame and power which are in abundance in Egypt and Babylon – the twin platforms of the marketplace. The reason why God would flood the economies and governments of nations with His apostles is because He wants to exercise authority in these spheres. It is only when God exercises His authority that His kingdom can be established in these two spheres. Then the kingdom of God can knock down the kingdoms of the world and annex them for Heaven's Great Monarch. For already the kingdoms of this world have become the kingdom of our God and of His Christ (Revelation 11: 15)!

> **God sends apostles to the marketplace to preserve remnants and extend His salvation among the nations; and not primarily for fortune, fame and power which are in abundance in Egypt and Babylon - the twin platforms of the marketplace**

4

SPIRITSTORM

For ever since the creation of the world, His invisible nature and attributes, that is, His eternal power and divinity, have been made intelligible and clearly discernible in and through the things that have been made (His handiworks)
(Romans 1:20,AMP)

The invisible world may not be apparent, but it is parent to the visible world. The visible world is birthed by the invisible world. This is because God, the creator of all things, is Spirit (John 4:24). The lifespan of the invisible is eternal, while that of the visible is time-bound (2 Corinthians 4:18). So we can safely surmise that the unseen or invisible is spiritual while the seen or visible is physical.

The spiritual is original, while the physical is a derivative. The physical is a derivative of the spiritual. The relationship between the spiritual and physical is like electricity and an electric fan. Electricity powers the fan to visibly rotate its blade even though it cannot be seen. The word 'spirit' in Hebrew is *ruach*, and it means wind. One characteristic of the wind is that it can animate without being seen. It can be felt without being caught. When the wind blows through a still tree, it causes the tree's leaves and branches to move while it remains unseen. Such is the nexus between the physical and spiritual. The physical is animated by the spiritual.

> The invisible world may not be apparent, but it is parent to the visible world. The visible world is birthed by the invisible world.

I have said elsewhere that the physical is just the tip of the iceberg while the bulk of the ice couches in the realm spiritual. It's like the internet today in which the surface web (popular web pages and websites that can be crawled and indexed by popular search engines) only makes up about 4%-10% of the net. At the same time, the deep and dark web (which cannot be crawled and indexed by popular search engines and which is home to computer geniuses of the wild ilk) makes up about 90%-96% of the entire web. Can you imagine that all the giant strides achieved with social media, e-commerce and search mostly fall in the surface web (4%-10% categories)? If this is the case, can you now imagine the advanced level of computing that takes place in the deep and dark web?*

This is why you cannot define an ocean by the slew of

---

*https://blog.knowbe4.com/what-is-the-difference-between-the-surface-web-the-deep-web-and-the-dark-web
https://scsuwisewords.wordpress.com/2015/06/24/beneath-the-surface-the-deep-web

boisterous vortices created by its surface waves. Oceans are defined by how deep and wide they are. So it is with the world – you cannot accurately judge things from the flurry of activities in the natural – you must go to the source of it all: the spiritual!

> the physical is just the tip of the iceberg while the bulk of the ice couches in the realm spiritual

THE SOCIAL ARCHITECTURE OF THE WORLD SYSTEM

By design, spiritual realities dwarf the physical by incalculable margins. This is why spirits are always involved as one climbs up the ladder. As far as people systems go, which is essentially what the social architecture of the world is about; it is impossible to make it to the top without the aid of a spirit. This is because the advanced architecture and engineering by which the physical is powered do not take place in the physical, which is merely an interface. They take place in the power source in which the source code is rooted in the spiritual.

> By design, spiritual realities dwarf the physical by incalculable margins. This is why spirits are always involved as one climbs up the ladder.

In the marketplace, whether in economy or government, it is impossible to make it to the top without the empowerment of a spirit. It is for this reason Joseph and Daniel maintained their consecration to God, without whom it would have been impossible for them to get to the top. This was why those that truly wielded power and influence in both Babylon and Egypt were either with God or other gods.

Let me state the obvious: it is impossible to make it to the top in any walk of life without the help of a spirit. There is no billionaire, star athlete, star entertainer, leader of thought, ace politician etc., who has made it without the aid of a spirit. Don't be deceived by the litany of well-edited and embellished rags-to-riches success stories that emphasise human efforts such as hard work, perseverance, dedication etc., without mentioning dedication to extraterrestrial forces of spiritual provenance.

Why is it impossible to make it to the very top of the marketplace of the nations without the aid of a spirit? It is because the physical world, as we have already established, is a derivative of the spiritual one – the visible world was framed by the invisible God. This the Bible has incontestably asserted thus,

> **By faith we understand that the worlds [during the successive ages] were framed (fashioned, put in order, and equipped for their intended purpose) by the word of God, so that what we see was not made out of things which are visible.** (Hebrews 11:3, AMP)

The control towers, command structures and power loci of the visible world are buried deep in the world whose existence is beyond the eye level of mortal men. It is like the

> Let me state the obvious: it is impossible to make it to the top in any walk of life without the help of a spirit. There is no billionaire, star athlete, star entertainer, leader of thought, ace politician etc., who has made it without the aid of a spirit.

commercial electricity we enjoy in our homes: The source of it is far removed from us. In most cases, where electricity is produced is hundreds and thousands of miles away from our homes. So we have no control whatsoever over what powers all our electronic hardware. Why? We have no hand in its production; we are at the bottom of the value chain, which is consumption.

In the same vein, production does not happen in the physical. It only happens in the spiritual. What happens in the physical is retail and consumption – selling and buying. So the marketplace of the nations, therefore, becomes the place where power sources are retailed and consumed. Those who wield the most power are they that have an intimate knowledge and operational know-how of their spirit support system. This is why the Bible says,

> *Exploits in the marketplace are wrought by those who have a direct, personal connection, commitment and devotion to a spirit by covenant*

> *...the people who know their God shall prove themselves strong and shall stand firm and do exploits* (Daniel 11:32, AMP).

Note that the knowledge spoken of in the verse of Scripture quoted above is more experiential than it is mental. Exploits in the marketplace are wrought by those who have a direct, personal connection, commitment and devotion to a spirit by covenant.

On the ladder of success in the marketplace, only a few notches can be climbed by hard work, education, training, expertise and all such things that can be acquired by human effort. There is a level human labour cannot climb beyond. It is at such a point that the upward transportation service and leadership of a spirit are required. This is true for all walks of life as figured in all the people systems under the heaven.

The social architecture of the world system is in this wise:

It is true that the spiritual controls the physical. It is, however also true that the creature that has been wired and designed by God to seamlessly connect these two realms is man. This is why no spirit, no matter how powerful, can directly operate on earth without the partnership of man. And why God and the devil require man's cooperation to bring forth their agenda on earth. Man is tripartite (consisting of spirit, soul and body according to 1 Thessalonians 5:23). His components uniquely enable him to touch the spiritual and the natural realms simultaneously.

Therefore, the social architecture of the world system is based on the tripartite nature of man and what part is most exercised. There are varying degrees of power the body, soul and spirit of man can handle, with the highest being the spirit in that order.

Brainstormers (Bottom Dwellers)

The brainstormers are those who elect to use their brain to figure out their lives. They put absolute trust in their brainpower; they 'brain storm', which is a term that refers to investing a lot of brainpower in solving life's problems. They are cerebral! They try to interpret everything in the world through what makes sense to their five senses - which is essentially everything that consists of the physical world. Anything that does not fit into the construct of the physical world and that cannot be interpreted by the facts and figures that *make sense* is treated with corpulent disdain. They are said to be smart!

In all fairness to this category of people, the good Lord sure did invest a lot in making the human brain an absolute marvel. Breakthroughs in neuroscience reveal dizzying information on the capacity and capabilities of the human brain. For instance, researchers reported that:

As powerful as the human brain is, the power it generates is only good enough for the bottom of the marketplace of nations

'According to a 2010 article in *Scientific American*, the memory capacity of the human brain was reported to have the equivalent of 2.5 *petabytes* of memory capacity.

As a number, a "*petabyte*" means 1024 terabytes or a million gigabytes, so the average adult human brain has the ability to store the equivalent of 2.5 *million gigabytes* of digital memory.

To put that in perspective, according to Computerworld, Yahoo – the Internet giant – has created a specially-built 2.0 *petabyte* "data warehouse". Yahoo uses the immense information storage capacity of this data warehouse to analyze the behaviour of its half-a-billion monthly visitors. "It is not only the world's single-largest database but also the busiest", the magazine reported.

By comparison, the IRS's massive data warehouse, which keeps track of 300-plus million Americans and many more million businesses, has the capacity of 150 *terabytes* of memory.

Yet Yahoo's 2.0-*petabyte* computational centre, which can process 24 billion "events" a day, is a full 20 per cent smaller than the capacity of a single human brain.

The human brain is indeed a marvel, with more capabilities than most of us can imagine. As more studies are coming out – it is only a matter of time until we truly find out how much the human brain can store[1].

> As powerful as the human brain is, the power it generates is only good enough for the bottom of the marketplace of nations.

One petabyte is the same as 20 million four-drawer filing cabinets filled with text, 13.3 years of HD-TV recordings, 4.7 billion books or 670 million web pages[2].

As powerful as the human brain is, the power it generates is only good enough for the bottom of the marketplace of nations. As we shall shortly see, the most significant solutions and inventions in the world do not originate from the human brain; they are spawned by spirit intelligence. Spirit intelligence is higher than the creativity of the most hyperconscious mind and super-intelligence of the most complex computer systems. This is why being smart alone does not translate to success in the marketplace; and many times, key players in the marketplace are not always smarter than those under them. Brain-power can be acquired by synergistic leveraging, but spirit intelligence is only available on a direct, one-on-one encounter with a spirit.

---

[1] *www.cnsnevada.com/what-is-the-memory-capacity-of-a-human-brain/*
[2] *www.telegraph.co.uk/news/science/science-news/12114150/Human-brain-can-store-4.7-billion-books-ten-times-more-than-originally-thought.html*

Soul searchers (Middle Dwellers)

The soul searchers are those who understand what Watchman Nee calls the *latent power of the soul* and conscientiously engage and harness it to make the most of it. These folks understand that there is something higher than brain power – the power of the soul. The power of the soul is like dry wood that needs to be set ablaze; it is like cold water that must be boiled to make tea – you need to constantly engage this power to get the best out of it. Consequently, those who engage the soul's latent power practice all sorts of techniques ranging from transcendental meditation, to astral travel (projection), to taking of hard drugs and stimulants in order to search out and utilise the power hidden in the soul's core.

> The soul searchers explore, excavate and fully exploit self. Most eastern, new age religions and indeed philosophical groups in the world belong in this category.

The core power of the soul is imagination. This power is so great that God Himself said whatever it grasps can physically manifest. Whatever man imagines can be converted to something tangible (Genesis 11:6).

The soul searchers explore, excavate and fully exploit self. Most eastern, new age religions and indeed philosophical groups in the world belong in this category. Much of art, entertainment and popular culture are driven by folks in this category. They are intermediaries between the brainstormers and spiritstormers. They are not too shallow to belong with the brainstormers but not too deep to belong with the spiritstormers. Hence, they are middle dwellers. While the brain's power is somewhat measurable, the soul's latent power - with imagination at its core cannot be measured, no, not by any human parameter or metric. So we can comparatively state that: the brain can be likened to a river, the soul can be compared to the sea, while the spirit can be likened to the ocean.

> We can comparatively state that the brain can be likened to a river, the soul can be compared to a sea, while the spirit can be likened to an ocean.

Spiritstormers (Upper Dwellers)
The spiritstormers directly connect with spirits to wield powers that go beyond and outside the reach of man's faculties. Whereas the brainstormers and soul searchers try to make the most of powers locked within man's frame, the spiritstormers totally defer to spirits in order to gain access to powers and wisdom that enable the spiritual to dwarf the natural. Also, just as the brainstormers and soul searchers are mostly confined to the tip of the iceberg, spiritstormers are granted unrestricted access to the bulk of the ice buried in the deep.

Most of the activities engaged in by soul searchers are influenced directly or tangentially by the spiritstormers while most of the activities that are being engaged in by the brainstormers are directly or tangentially influenced by the soul searchers.

Spiritstormers utilise the search facility within their spirits and directly explore and interface with the spiritual. From here, they progress to directly engaging a spirit entity. The spirit entity, in turn, imbues them with wisdom and power to dominate their immediate environment. By so doing, they access wisdom and power that transcend the four corners of the earth. They receive revelations beyond the carrying capacity of the brain and the soul. Oh yes, things beyond the processing power of the mind and the expansive reach of the imagination.

> **The spiritstormers directly connect with spirits to wield powers that go beyond and outside the reach of man's faculties.**

The Christian life is not rooted in the brain or the soul; it is rooted in the spirit as it is joined to the Spirit of God. For the Christian, the spirit entity that guides them into their adventure in the spiritual is the Holy Spirit. The centre and circumference of the Christian's adventure in the spirit is Christ in God (Colossians 3:3). The Holy Spirit is the sole custodian and dispenser of everything about God through Christ, even His wisdom and power. This is why the Bible says,

> **Now unto him that is able to do exceeding abundantly above all that we ask or think, according to the power that worketh in us** (Ephesians 3:20, KJV).

Of course, the power at work in the believer does not originate from the believer and does not originate from any other spirit apart from the uncreated Spirit of God!

The Christian faith system has been designed to empower every believer to become a spirit-stormer. At salvation the believer's spirit is quickened and joined to the Spirit of God in a mystical union. The Bible confirms this thus:

> *But he that is joined unto the Lord is one spirit.*
> (1 Corinthians 6:17, KJV)

The union between the believer's spirit and God's Spirit forms the basis of the relationship between the believer and God. As the believer exercises their faith in communion – prayer, study and obedience, they gain access to increasing measures of God's wisdom and power. It is impossible for man to search out and explore God. That is why the Holy Spirit helps the believer plunge into God and gain ascendancy in Him. The actual searching is done by the Holy Spirit. This is why the Bible says,

> *But God has revealed them to us through His Spirit. FOR THE SPIRIT SEARCHES ALL THINGS, YES, THE DEEP THINGS OF GOD. For what man knows the things of a man except the spirit of the man which is in him? Even so no one knows the things of God except the Spirit of God. Now we have received, not the spirit of the world, but the Spirit who is from God, that we might know the things that have been freely given to us by God* (1 Corinthians 2:10-12, NKJV)

Note that the Spirit of God resident in the believer searches the depth of God and the depth of man. The Bible says,

> *The spirit of a man is the lamp of the Lord, searching all the inner depths of his heart.*
> (Proverbs 20:27, NKJV)

So, the Holy Spirit effectively and concurrently mines the flawless wealth of God's depths and excavates the believer's depth thereby, filling the believer's depth with the wealth of God's depth.

> The Christian life is not rooted in the brain or the soul; it is rooted in the spirit as it is joined to the Spirit of God. For the Christian, the spirit entity that guides them into their adventure in the spiritual is the Holy Spirit.

Just as the believer is joined to the Lord and becomes one spirit with the Lord, an unbeliever can be joined to a demon spirit and become one spirit with the demon; this is called *demon possession*. The unbeliever is said to be possessed by a demon. And just the way the Lord's power and wisdom flow to the believer by the instrumentality of their spirit, so do demonic wisdom and power flow to the unbeliever through the instrumentality of their spirit. The spirit of man is a lamp in the hands of the Lord but an instrument of darkness in the devil's hands.

A believer cannot be possessed (because they are already joined to the Lord and have become one spirit with the Lord) but can be subject to demonic torment any time they break the hedge of righteousness. This is called *demonization*. For he that breaks the hedge, a serpent will bite him (Ecclesiastes 10:8). This is why some believers, though free in Christ, still grapple with demonic onslaughts, limitations and disadvantages.

Note, however, that not all adversities that a believer experiences are demon-controlled – especially those that are not tied in any way to their disobedience. Some are permitted by God to glorify Himself in the believer's life or address an issue or two in their lives. For example, Job's case was not demonization because God permitted it; and the devil was strictly instructed not to touch Job's soul (Job 1:12). The worst the devil could do was to mangle Job's flesh and everything else that was externally linked to him. Paul also had a messenger of Satan, which buffeted his flesh to keep him humble (2 Corinthians 12:7). So, in this case, the devil was only in the picture (as an item), but God was the painter.

Back to the matter of demon possession. An unbeliever who is joined in spirit with a demon spirit(s) is either used as a medium (as in the case of the slave girl possessed by the spirit of divination in Acts 16:16); or tormented till they become like a vegetable, (as in the case of the mad man of Gadarea, who was possessed by a legion of demons in Mark 5:1-9). Now, demonic spiritstormers are those who are used as mediums to convey demonic wisdom and power. These include founders of religions and occultic organisations: spirit channelers like JZ Knight; Alice Bailey (whose work shaped much of what we know as the United Nations); Helena Blavatsky (co-founder of the occultic organisation called Theosophical Society); Maharishi Mahesh Yogi (the developer of the Transcendental Meditation Technique whose disciples included top tier pop culture icons and many millions today); Marie Laveau (who

> Human civilisation has been shaped by the work of spiritstormers - believers and unbelievers alike. Spiritstormers partner with spirit entities and tap into the spirit realities of supernatural civilisations and import them into the earth.

singlehandedly hauled Voodoo from its West African cradle and established it in the United States). Others include, Margaret Sanger (the founder of Planned Parenthood, an organisation known for masterminding and overseeing the slaughter of millions of unborn babies in the name of abortion around the world); Karl Marx (the social engineer and philosopher whose work literally sought to expunge God from society and polarised the world into two ideological blocks); Charles Darwin (who tried to prove the non-existence of God by using science), inventors, captains of industry etc. It is practically impossible to make a comprehensive list of demonic spiritstormers past and present without needing the space for volumes of books. We have to remain within the orbit of our discourse.

Human civilisation has been shaped by the work of spiritstormers believers and unbelievers alike. Spiritstormers partner with spirit entities and tap into the spirit realities of supernatural civilisations and import them into the earth. For the believer, their work imports the kingdom of heaven to earth. For the unbeliever, their work imports the kingdom of darkness to earth. Every walk of life that is figured within the ambit of the marketplace is manned and commandeered by spiritstormers – people who know how to operate by spirit intelligence.

THE FIGHT IS NOT WITH HUMAN VESSELS BUT WITH SPIRIT ENTITIES

Every people system has a spirit gatekeeper that must be contended with, overcome and bound before the believer can successfully execute their God-given assignment. Otherwise, the believer would toil in an endless streak of frustration with little or nothing to show for it. The believer would be tilted in error to strike amiss while the devil keeps increasing his wins.

Jesus emphatically said,

> *How can one enter a strong man's house and plunder his goods, unless he first binds the strong man? And then he will plunder his house* (Matthew 12:29, NKJV)

Every apostle of God in the marketplace must know this fundamental truth: that God's message would not be delivered in the marketplace by friendly consultation but by militant confrontation in the spirit. The primary reason for being sent to the marketplace is not for banquets, but conquest. The 'strong men' of the marketplace do not respond to reasonable negotiations. They only respond to superior wisdom and power that can

> **Every people system has a spirit gatekeeper that must be contended with, overcome and bound before the believer can successfully execute their God-given assignment.**

only be exclusively supplied by God and appropriated by those who have accepted His lordship.

In the marketplace of nations, believers' victories are tied to how well they bind the strong men of their portion of the marketplace. As a believer who God has called to represent Him in the marketplace, you should know that your certificates, work experience, money, power, human connections and every other such thing are not enough to bind the strong men of your portion of the marketplace. They can only at best be used as appurtenances to enhance your conquest. Your victory does not emanate from anyone or anything on earth. Your victory comes in the name of the Lord – underpinned by the authority of the Highest!

The 'strong men' in the marketplace are not human. They are spirit entities! In the demonic chain of command, human beings are just the interfaces, portals and vehicles. Humans are mere comptrollers; the real controllers and manufacturers of the goods are enthroned in the unseen realm, whose authority must be challenged and vanquished for God's agenda to prosper in the marketplace. This is why Paul strategically said,

> **For we are not wrestling with flesh and blood [contending only with physical opponents], but against the despotisms, against the powers, against [the master spirits who are] the world rulers of this present darkness, against the spirit forces of wickedness in the heavenly (supernatural) sphere.** (Ephesians 6:12, AMP)

You see, ours is not a fight with the *tip of the iceberg*. We are meant to wage war against the nefarious shenanigans of the *bulk of ice* buried in the deep. We do not have business having a scrimmage with the human beings who are more or less puppets in a grand master plan. We are to contend with spirits that dole out the skewed marching orders by which the human elements operate.

Now, in the warfare for apostolic conquests in the marketplace, God's apostles in the marketplace are not the ones doing the fighting in the real sense of it; they are weapons in God's hands. A weapon only does the bidding of the fighter. God Himself said,

> ***Thou art* MY BATTLE AXE AND WEAPONS OF WAR:** *for with thee will I break in pieces the nations, and with thee will I destroy kingdoms* (Jeremiah 51:20, KJV, emphasis added)

When God wields His battle axes on the plantations of darkness, He does not aim for the stems, branches or leaves. He aims for the roots! This is why John the Baptist said,

> *... The axe is laid unto the root of the trees...* (Matthew 3:10, KJV)

The roots of a tree are not readily visible to the human eye, but therein lay the source of life and vitality for the tree. In context, roots signify the hidden life and source of power and wisdom by which demonic systems and installations are established and run. So, when God lays His battle axes on the roots of these demonic trees, He is delivering the coup de grace - a sort of destruction that does not even leave behind ashes for reference and memories. Therefore, God's strategy for apostolic conquest is to deal with the roots of evil which are invariably traceable to evil

> The 'strong men' in the marketplace are not human. They are spirit entities! In the demonic chain of command, human beings are just the interfaces, portals and vehicles. Human beings are mere comptrollers; the real controllers and manufacturers of the goods are enthroned in the unseen realm

spirits. This is tied to two things:

- The believer's priesthood by which deep-seated intercession is cultivated, nurtured and established. It is as simple as this: no intercession, no apostolic conquest.
- The believer's daily bearing of the cross of Jesus Christ which ensures daily victory over themselves is achieved and by which the power of a pure life is drawn upon to daily discomfit the prince of the world – the devil. This is what consecration is about. An unconsecrated believer would end up being a casualty in the war for apostolic conquest in the marketplace.

> When God lays His battle axes on the roots of these demonic trees, He is delivering the coup de grace - a sort of destruction that does not even leave behind ashes for reference and memories.

ALTARS AND SPIRITS

An altar is a place where the natural and spiritual confluence. It is a shaft that bridges the gap between and connects the visible to the invisible so that there can be a direct exchange between the two realms. An altar is a place where spirit intelligence, content, wisdom and power are conveyed for onward use, execution and establishment in the natural.

The blueprint of the tabernacle that God gave Moses was meant to be executed flawlessly (Exodus 25:9). The tabernacle was meant to host God's presence. But to successfully host God's presence, it had to be constructed exactly as it was revealed in terms of dimensions and measurements. The dimensions were given to give no room for human error. The dimensions and measurements of the tabernacle clearly reveal spirit

> An altar is a place where the natural and spiritual confluence. It is a shaft that bridges the gap between and connects the visible to the invisible so that there can be a direct exchange between the two realms.

intelligence. These dimensions would also ensure that the gap between heaven and earth was bridged and the natural and spiritual would confluence. The tabernacle Moses built accurately modelled the one in heaven so that there would be no difference between heaven and earth. And when Moses finished the work, God filled the tabernacle with His glory in a sight that proved a seamless connection between heaven and earth, the visible and the invisible (Exodus 40:33-34)!

The first person to build an altar unto the Lord in the entire Bible was Noah in Genesis 8:20. Abraham, the patriarch of faith, was a man of the altar. His walk with God was characterised by altars. Almost every milestone of his journey of faith was marked by the building of an altar. Genesis 12:7-8; 13:4, 18; 22:9 confirms this. Abraham passed this legacy of building altars unto the Lord to his son Isaac who passed it to his son Jacob, and this would become the culture of the nation that would eventuate from this legacy of faith.

At a functional altar, the material seamlessly connects with the immaterial, and man meets spirit. The man is saddled with the responsibility of making the altar conducive for the frequent visit of the spirit through elaborate rituals, sacrifices and activities that are usually revealed by the spirit to the man. The man is also supposed to maintain certain conducts, routines and disciplines that would make him worthy of being a host to the spirit. Every altar is built to host some spirit(s).

Altars, especially as they had to do with hosting the Spirit of God in the Old Testament, were primarily physical pieces, articles and spaces built in tandem with the design of God. In the New Testament, God has shifted all operations to the recreated spirit of man. Oh yes, He no longer dwells in temples made with human hands (Acts 7:48). He has permanently relocated from physical temples, tabernacles and altars into the recreated human spirit (1 Corinthians 3:16). At salvation, the first thing that happens is: God makes the spirit of man His new residence to build a home and have communion with the believer.

> At a functional altar, the material seamlessly connects with the immaterial, and man meets spirit.

I stated early on in this book that the devil and demons are incapable of having a relationship with man. They can only at best transact. So when they possess a human vessel by latching on to their spirit, they do not settle in to make a home or have communion like God. Instead, they hang onto the human spirit like parasites who only use the human vessel to further their cause and achieve their goals. So demons can only at best make a medium out of the human vessels they possess. Their operation within a human vessel always shreds the human soul to pieces. They use the human vessel in such a way that the person hosting them ends up losing.

> Satan is a created being therefore; his wisdom and power are finite. Satan is nowhere near God in terms of operational sophistication.

Satan is a created being therefore; his wisdom and power are finite. Satan is nowhere near God in terms of operational sophistication. So, demonic altars are still largely figured in the physical – this includes amulets, demonic temples, shrines, tattoos, totems, enchantments from dark texts or dark oral bequests, angular alignments with the constellations, human, animal and plant sacrifices, specially designed articles etc. More on the operation of demons is a matter altogether for another book.

THE FIRST THING YOU SHOULD DO IS BUILD AN ALTAR

Apostleship in the marketplace is defined and shaped by the clarity of purpose and assignment that fire a sense of urgency in the believer's heart. The wisdom and power of God embodied in and dispensed by Christ (1 Corinthians 1:24) are the two resources an apostle in the marketplace needs to function well. The believer lives each day with a sent mentality within their allotted sphere in the marketplace. They make the most of all opportunities to deliver the message by preaching Christ crucified in words and deeds.

No people system is impossible to penetrate, no matter how seemingly impregnably fortified. By prophetic insight, God reveals the system's weaknesses and fault lines and lineaments to the apostle and imbues them with wisdom to infiltrate them and the power to exploit them. Often, this happens when a problem breaks out in a sphere that God has sufficiently trained and armed the apostle to function. In most cases, the apostle would have a complete grasp of the solution. Joseph and Daniel are good examples.

> Now, the first thing a believer should do after obeying the call to take over a sphere of the marketplace is to build an altar.

Now, the first thing a believer should do after obeying the call to take over a sphere of the marketplace is to build an altar. In the Old Testament, altars were physical structures built with the aid and guide of spirit intelligence to bridge the gap between the spiritual and the natural. In the New Testament, however, altars are holy routines, regiments, and activities that a believer observes (as underpinned by God's instruction) and galvanises with strong consecration to make more room for the indwelling presence of the Spirit to saturate them and for the manifest presence of God to saturate their workspace. This requires discipline. A believer without discipline is not a profitable disciple of Jesus Christ.

For instance, God could instruct a believer to pray for a certain amount of time and at a specific time in the day for their office, place of business etc. Sometimes He might even choose not to tell the believer why. As long as this person continues in obedience, an altar is set up. And how we know there is an altar is that God fills the office, place of business etc., with His manifest presence. Anytime God shows up in His manifest presence, demonic installations are decimated and cancelled. God's manifest presence is the only potent demon expellant. Unlike God's altar, which is fully figured within the human vessel and purely spiritual, demonic altars still heavily depend on physical articles and structures to function.

Note that setting up and servicing an altar unto God increases the believer's capacity to imbibe more of God and represent Him accurately in the marketplace. The continued engagement and expansion of the indwelling presence of God within the believer *cleans them* up and rids them of character flaws, habits etc., that demon spirits can latch on to so as to afflict them. While the manifest presence of God arms them with the ability to execute God's will in the given people system He has sent them to take over in His name.

PRACTICAL APPLICATION OF ALTARS IN THE MARKETPLACE: MY CASE

In my over fifteen years of active kingdom service as an apostle of Jesus Christ in the marketplace, I have witnessed, firsthand, the power and importance of raising an altar. Two years after I was employed in the Petroleum Products Pricing and Regulatory Agency (PPPRA), a federal government organisation charged with the responsibility of ensuring that the supply, consumption and pricing of petroleum products in Nigeria are properly kept in check, I was transferred from my first station to another city and saddled with the responsibility of oversight. As soon as I arrived, two things immediately drew my attention:

1. There was a potent demonic altar that had been set up, which unleashed shock wave after shock wave of afflictions.

I remember one of my colleagues got to the office one morning and got paralysed as soon as he sat in his chair. I heard that others before him either lost their lives or were left with terrible illnesses. Others sought redeployment immediately upon resumption in order to escape the nameless raging plague in my office. I knew running away was not an option because it was the Lord who sent me there. Therefore, I immediately sought the Lord's face in prayer and fasting on what to do. The Lord came through and showed me the man responsible for servicing the demonic altar. He opened my eyes to see that the man in question cast evil spells through seemingly benign handshakes. I continued to shake hands with him as I kept decimating the demonic altar in the name of the Lord. The altar was destroyed, and in a few months, the man was gone. Glory to God!

2. The administrative structure by which my office was run was fraught with corruption of epidemic proportions. I mean, every aspect of our official operations was tainted by unrighteousness. The people who had handed over to us had elected to make filthy lucre from what was meant to be a straightforward operation – they had made a fortune by charging for services meant to be free, for example. So, upon resuming our official duties, we were confronted with the onerous task of literally making the *crooked paths straight*.

I immediately knew that my team could only win by righteousness if we were serious about any form of apostolic conquest. This time we would have to match deep-seated intercession with practical godliness. Like Daniel's comrades, we would have to damn the consequences and refuse to bow to the image of gold.

By the grace of God, we reversed the unrighteous decision made by our predecessors to charge for stamps on all documents that passed through my office. Stamps were meant to be free, and this was what we made them – no more charges. When the news spread that my office no longer charged for stamps, we were deemed to have gone nuts. However, we knew that by this singular action, we had broken the power of mammon and made room for God's kingdom to invade and take over my office space. Because you cannot serve God and mammon at the same time!

> We raised an altar unto the Lord right in my office where the incense of prayer daily ascended to heaven. We did not shut down work to pray as this would have contravened the principle of righteousness by which we stood!

Great grace was released upon my team to even do more in the name of the Lord. We raised an altar unto the Lord right in my office where the incense of prayer daily ascended to heaven. We did not shut down work to pray as this would have contravened the principle of righteousness by which we stood! We set the coordinates of each day by prayer, utilised every free time to draw strength from the Lord in prayer, and sharpened ourselves up in active fellowship with one another during breaks. We simply remodelled our office space for the exclusive occupancy of the Most Holy One of Zion! The manifest presence of God so saturated my office that there was no space left for any demonic influence to penetrate. I replicated this in every station I was transferred to.

As I climbed up the management ladder, I got swarmed with greater temptations, but the grace of God helped me to reject each opportunity to be disloyal to my king. For me, the peak of it was when some oil merchants dropped a sizeable bag stuffed with bundles of hundred dollar bills to bribe me if I would agree to falsify records. I lie not, the notes were crispy, and the scent electrified the senses by sending mammonic chills down the spine. The people offering it had mastered the art of making irresistible offers. They were very Machiavellian, so saying no to them also subtly meant jeopardising my life. But then, I knew that my portion of the marketplace could only be conquered by righteousness (as I believe is the case with every inch of the marketplace of the nations). The apostolic conquest would be compromised if I stooped so low to accept kickbacks.

The Lord would eventually show mercy by helping me reach out to folks in my sphere of the marketplace that would have otherwise been impossible to reach. Soon, colleagues and superiors alike, sometimes from different faiths, would reach out to me with problems that defied all human solutions and ask me to pray to my God for answers. The Lord did come through mightily all the times – there were healings, deliverances and breakthroughs precipitated by the wisdom and power of God. The signs, seals and strengths of my apostleship in my office became reinforced with the unblemished testimony of Christ that

I upheld by grace. And, yes, I became known as 'Pastor', not as a generic title but as an apostolic marker.

5

STRIKE AND SPARE NOT

Elisha had become sick with the illness of which he would die. Then Joash the king of Israel came down to him, and wept over his face, and said, "O my father, my father, the chariots of Israel and their horsemen!" And Elisha said to him, "Take a bow and some arrows." So he took himself a bow and some arrows. Then he said to the king of Israel, "Put your hand on the bow." So he put his hand on it, and Elisha put his hands on the king's hands. And he said, "Open the east window"; and he opened it. Then Elisha said, "Shoot"; and he shot. And he said, "The arrow of the Lord's deliverance and the arrow of deliverance from Syria; for you must strike the Syrians at Aphek till you have destroyed them." Then he said, "Take the arrows"; so he took them. And he said to the king of Israel, "Strike the ground"; so he struck three times, and stopped. And the man of God *was angry with him, and said, "You should have struck five or six times; then you would have struck Syria till you had destroyed it! But now you will strike Syria only three times."* (2 Kings 13:14-19, NKJV)

The above passage contains the last act of Elisha as God's prophet before he was gathered unto his fathers in death.

Joash, the king of Israel, would not let Elisha transit to the great beyond without first drawing some last virtue from the prophet of God who had inherited the double portion of Elijah's spirit. King Joash tearfully echoed the same cry Elisha had made when Elijah was about to be wheeled off the earth by chariots of fire. Elisha understood what his cry meant and decided to get right to the business of attending to the king.

At the time of the encounter in the passage above, Syria was a thorn in Israel's side. The prophet of God had marshalled the resources of heaven to rid Israel of Syria before leaving the earth. But he would entrust the execution of the judgement of Syria into King Joash's hands, literally!

First, King Joash was asked to shoot the arrow of the Lord's deliverance and the arrow of the deliverance from Syria through the east window. This, he did flawlessly.

Second, King Joash was asked again to take some arrows and strike the ground. He struck the ground three times. The prophet of God was angry that King Joash only struck three times because the number of times he hit the ground would translate to the number of victories Israel would have under his watch against Syria. And three times was not enough to annihilate Syria. He would have struck five or six times, that would have comprehensively sealed Syria's doom. King Joash struck but sparingly. The consequence would mean an inconclusive victory – at the end of the day, there would be no net win! Israel was short-changed by her king, who struck sparingly in the day it mattered the most.

Note that Elisha died immediately after this. So, there was no room for correction and second chances.

WHAT THIS PRACTICALLY MEANS

Syria had been presented in a one-time offer for decimation to King Joash, but he got sloppy and spared while he struck. The importance of being thorough in execution was lost on him, so he squandered an opportunity to deliver his whole nation from the incessant assaults of Syria.

This is what happens when untrained, undiscipled people are sent forth like loose cannons on apostolic missions to the marketplace. Untrained hands loosely forge the deck that would eventually collapse into a heap of colossal mess.

Whether within the church or in the marketplace, the seal of apostleship is thorough conquest. This is seen in how many people submit to the lordship of Christ by the instrumentality of a person's apostolic ministry. Those who yield to training would in turn yield robust results that would stand the unrelenting fires of eternity. The seal of an apostle is carved by the number of people that get on their knees in surrender to the lordship of Jesus on account of their ministry (1 Corinthians 9:2). In the marketplace, this is seen by how the utilisation of the wisdom and power of God by an apostle in the marketplace gets the Nebuchadnezzars and Pharaohs of the world and those under them to bow down to Heaven's Great King.

> **Untrained hands loosely forge the deck that would eventually collapse into a heap of colossal mess.**

In our earlier study of Joseph and Daniel, I pointed out that they both underwent intensive training before they were released to function at full capacity. It is therefore impossible to do much in the name of the Lord without intensive training and discipline.

Training and discipline involve stretching and expanding one's capacity within the most inauspicious and inconvenient circumstances. The pavilion of convenience, otherwise known as the comfort zone, must be burnt to the ground for one to build a towering stature with God and command His blessings in the marketplace of the nations. The Bible says,

> **ENLARGE** *the place of thy tent, and let them* **STRETCH FORTH** *the curtains of thine habitations:* **SPARE NOT, LENGTHEN** *thy cords, and* **STRENGTHEN** *thy stakes* (Isaiah 54:2, KJV, emphasis added)

The words and phrases emphasised in the verse of Scripture are basically verbs of almost militant categorisation. This verse of Scripture very well captures the essence of training and discipline.

> Training and discipline involve stretching and expanding one's capacity within the most inauspicious and inconvenient circumstances. The pavilion of convenience, otherwise known as the comfort zone, must be burnt to the ground for one to build a towering stature with God and command His blessings in the marketplace of the nations.

The training and discipline I speak of are not mechanical, man-engineered, ascetic and stoical routines that produce only a form of godliness utterly bereft of the power and wisdom of God. I am talking about the training and discipline of the Spirit. This helps us accept the government of God and function with a full understanding of His economy. This builds us into stewards who are deft at taking orders from God and making the most of all resources entrusted to us; thereby, putting the soul-refining heat and pressure in us until true character is unshakeably formed within us.

The training and discipline of the Spirit are administered by the Holy Spirit and those he has given the grace to beget us in the gospel. A believer who yields to God's training and discipline would not disobey God; would be faithful in executing God's instructions to the last jot, and would not squander God-given resources. They would thoroughly execute the will of God in their sphere of influence, thereby giving the devil no space at all to function. They will strike and spare not!

Each time we half-heartedly execute God's will either out of sheer carelessness or outright disobedience, we lose vital kingdom ground to the devil. King Saul struck and spared the Amalekites in outright disobedience to God and lost the kingdom as a direct consequence (1 Samuel 15:22-23).

THE NEED FOR TRAINING AND DISCERNING THE BODY

Apostles must fully yield to the Lord's training because they are surely going to need it in the coming days. A day of reckoning would surely come when what they have learnt from the Lord would be put to the test. It is not in God's character to initiate training on the job. Absolutely not! He trains before giving the job, but He expands and increases the one He has trained on the job. Before David had his golden moment with Goliath, he had been trained by the Lord in the wilderness. During David's training under God, the Lord furnished a quiet confidence in his heart in His omnipotence, eternal reliability and dependability. It was the unflinching confidence that David had in the Lord and the Lord's impartations in his life that made him refuse to step into another man's armour and use another man's sword in the day of battle. The Lord's training empowered David to be deft and proficient with the sling. And in the day it mattered the most, a whole nation was delivered from the brink of destruction when his training under the Lord was put to the test. David would go on to testify in one of the Psalms thus:

> ***Blessed be the Lord my Rock, Who trains my hands for war, and my fingers for battle*** (Psalm 144:1, NKJV)

Before the church was born, God directly trained men in the wilderness and sent them to declare His counsel to a generation,

> **Apostles must fully yield to the Lord's training because they are surely going to need it in the coming days.**

execute His will and carry out an assignment in His name. This was largely the norm in the Old Testament. The last man who also doubled as the last vestige of this old paradigm was John the Baptist. This old paradigm was discontinued as soon as the church was born upon the death and resurrection of Jesus Christ.

God set up an authority structure within the church (known as the body of Christ) with Christ as the head to handle the training of all believers for the work of the ministry. Now, God seldom sends men to the wilderness to be trained by Him. With the new paradigm, He has, through the election of grace, delegated authority within the body of Christ to ensure there is divine order and coordination among the saints. When the parts of the body work harmoniously together, there is growth and nourishment. When they do not, there is gangrene, disease and death. The Bible says,

> *...holding fast to the Head, from Whom the entire body, supplied and knit together by means of its joints and ligaments, grows with a growth that is from God.* (Colossians 2:19, AMP)

By design, the church is the epitome of order, coordination and synergy. Isolationism is taboo and attracts deathly consequences. The apostolic ministry, whether within the church or in the marketplace draws upon the extant order, synergy and coordination in the church which in turn draws upon the eternal order, coordination and synergy in the Godhead. The Bible clearly explains actual order, synergy and coordination in the church as follows:

> It was the unflinching confidence that David had in the Lord and the Lord's impartations in his life that made him refuse to step into another man's armour and use another man's sword in the day of battle.

For as the body is one and has many members, but all the members of that one body, being many, are one body, so also is Christ. For by one Spirit we were all baptized into one body — whether Jews or Greeks, whether slaves or free — and have all been made to drink into one Spirit. For in fact the body is not one member but many.

If the foot should say, "Because I am not a hand, I am not of the body," is it therefore not of the body? And if the ear should say, "Because I am not an eye, I am not of the body," is it therefore not of the body? If the whole body were an eye, where would be the hearing? If the whole were hearing, where would be the smelling? But now God has set the members, each one of them, in the body just as He pleased. And if they were all one member, where would the body be?

But now indeed there are many members, yet one body. And the eye cannot say to the hand, "I have no need of you"; nor again the head to the feet, "I have no need of you." No, much rather, those members of the body which seem to be weaker are necessary. And those members of the body which we think to be less honorable, on these we bestow greater honor; and our unpresentable parts have greater modesty, but our presentable parts have no need. But God composed the body, having given greater honor to that part which lacks it, that there should be no schism in the body, but that the members should have the same care for one another. And if one member suffers, all the members suffer with it; or if one member is honored, all the members rejoice with it.

Now you are the body of Christ, and members individually. And God has appointed these in the church: first apostles, second prophets, third teachers, after that miracles, then gifts of healings, helps, administrations, varieties of tongues. (1 Corinthians 12:12-28, NKJV)

Every believer is a member of the body of Christ. And one of the basic forms of training every member of the body of Christ should have is to *discern the body*. To discern the body means for a believer to supernaturally have a grasp of their place in the body: how connected they are to other believers and the need to constantly service this connection in communion for health, growth and life. Failure to do this results in

> God set up an authority structure within the church (known as the body of Christ) with Christ as the head to handle the training of all believers for the work of the ministry.

weakness, illness and death. (1 Corinthians 11:29-30)

In discerning the body, we must understand that as believers, we cannot thrive on our own. We must connect with other members of the body. We all indeed have eternal life, but there are certain supplies we cannot directly get from the Head (Christ) because He has already given it to some of our fellow believers. We can, therefore, only get these supplies when we connect with them in communion.

> By design, the church is the epitome of order, coordination and synergy. Isolationism is taboo and attracts deathly consequences.

Some would argue that Paul himself said as soon as he received his ministry to the Gentiles, he did not confer with flesh and blood, not even the apostles before him. And that upon receiving his ministry from the Lord, he immediately went up to the desert of Arabia where he spent a total of seventeen years to hone that which he received from the Lord (Galatians 1:17-24; 2:1-2).

The premise of this argument is flawed.

First, Paul was talking about the peculiarity and demands of his ministry (the target audience of which were the Gentiles) and not isolation and independence. Because the texture, structure and target audience of his ministry was different from those of the apostles before him, it behoved Paul to ensure there was no mixture of any kind. The Lord was pioneering something new through Paul, and he was ready and willing to give it all it would take. His sojourn in the desert of Arabia was for incubation and not for separation from the apostles before him.

Second, it is true that the Lord Jesus Christ encountered Saul (Paul) and no man had a hand in his conversion. Yet, he had to be introduced into the body life by Brother Ananias, whom the Lord instructed to pray for him so that his three-day blindness would come to an end, he would be filled with the Holy Spirit and be baptized (Acts 9:17-18). Oh yes, Paul's sight, getting filled with the Holy Ghost and baptism were put in Brother Ananias' hands – he surely could not do any of those things by himself. Even though he encountered the Lord Jesus directly, he had to receive the life supply that came through Brother Ananias. This was his first experience of the coordination, order and synergy within the body and would influence his understanding of the body life.

> To discern the body means for a believer to supernaturally have a grasp of their place in the body: how connected they are to other believers and the need to constantly service this connection in communion for health, growth and life. Failure to do this results in weakness, illness and death.

Third, even in faraway Arabia, Paul saw the need to touch base with the church in Jerusalem. He would establish contact with Peter and James, the Lord's brother (Galatians 1:18-19). And after the seventeen years were done, he submitted everything he had done in ministry to the apostles before him for review. Hear Paul out:

Fourteen years later I went up again to Jerusalem, this time with Barnabas. I took Titus along also. I went in response to a revelation and set before them the gospel that I preach among the Gentiles. But I did this privately to those who seemed to be leaders; for fear that I was running or had run my race in vain.

On the contrary, they saw that I had been entrusted with the task of preaching the gospel to the Gentiles, just as Peter had been to the Jews. For God, who was at work in the ministry of Peter as an apostle to the Jews, was also at work in my ministry as an apostle to the Gentiles. James, Peter and John, those reputed to be pillars, **GAVE ME AND BARNABAS THE RIGHT HAND OF FELLOWSHIP** when they recognized the grace given to me. **THEY AGREED** that we should go to the Gentiles, and they to the Jews. All they asked was that we should continue to remember the poor, the very thing I was eager to do (Galatians 2:1-2; 7-10, NIV, emphasis added).

This effectively put Paul in the same rank as the apostles before him. And like the apostles before him, they got their training directly from the Lord. But all those who would come after them would have to have been sons and daughters in the gospel to some brother or sister.

Paul submitted himself to the apostles before him because he knew how to discern the body and the importance of yielding to the delegated authority within the structure set up by God himself to administer the church.

I have said all this to say this: a believer whose ministry cannot be traced to that of another man or woman will surely be traced to the devil. You cannot say you have a ministry, and you do not have a history of tutelage and submission to the ministry of someone who has been in the faith before you. You cannot be effective without the life supply that comes through other believers. This is especially true in our day and time in which the church is about two thousand years. The church now is more structurally advanced than that of the days of the first apostles. This means you cannot be like Melchizedek, who had no known antecedents, parents, history etc. Some man or woman of God who was in the faith before you must have helped train and disciple you. It is impossible to have a ministry in isolation!

> Paul submitted himself to the apostles before him because he knew how to discern the body and the importance of yielding to the delegated authority within the structure set up by God himself to administer the church.

So, as an apostle of the Lord Jesus Christ in the marketplace, submitting to someone who was in the faith before you is critical - someone who can call you to both order and account. You can have as many instructors and mentors as possible (through books and tapes and even direct contact), but you must have someone you call father (or mother) in the gospel (1 Corinthians 4:15). Otherwise, your ministry would not receive the requisite life supply to make an impact in your sphere of influence -

> A believer whose ministry cannot be traced to that of another man or woman will surely be traced to the devil.

the marketplace. Not having a father in the gospel is the reason so many believers drift into error and have their whole assignments reverse-engineered by the wisdom and power of Satan. I must add that whoever you submit to must also be an ardent follower of Christ (1 Corinthians 11:1).

The Lord does not send untrained believers and does not put up with those who reject discipline.

EXECUTING THE LORD'S WILL WITH A SENSE OF URGENCY

It was David who said the king's business must be handled with haste (1 Samuel 21:8). Of course, the haste spoken of here is not that which is devoid of rigorous attention to detail and unflinching commitment to the thorough execution of a given task. No! It means promptness in obedience blended with great attention to detail. This surely requires a capacity that operates beyond the seams of human limitations.

The sent mentality that an apostle has should be complemented with a sense of urgency, always! This is crucial to note because most times, we mistake compliance for effectiveness. What differentiates a messenger of the cross of Jesus Christ in any sphere of human endeavour, but more especially in the marketplace, is divine urgency. This is the vigour, fervour and vitality constantly being supplied by the Holy Spirit with which Christ crucified is preached in word and deed.

Our hearts must remain constantly galvanised with the fire of His presence so that our words would burn the hearts of those who listen to us as our actions convict them. Our Lord and

Master Jesus Christ modelled this mode of operation to us as follows:

- Strangers testified of their hearts burning as with fire while Jesus spoke with them. The Bible says,

  And they said one to another; did not our heart burn within us, while he talked with us by the way, and while he opened to us the scriptures? (Luke 24:32, KJV)

- The Bible calls Jesus Christ the Amen (literally the *So Be It*) of God (Revelation 3:14). He did not only do the Father's will. He embodied the flawless, prompt, and thorough execution of God's will, thereby becoming the template for the complete execution of God's will amid the most extreme contradictions. Especially the likes of which are endemic to the marketplace. John the Baptist prophesied that Jesus would baptise with the Holy Ghost and with fire (Mathew 3:11)! Let's receive this baptism daily. The Holy Ghost refreshes and enlivens us while the fire continually keeps our chambers ablaze for executing God's will promptly everywhere, even in the undulating, treacherous terrains of the marketplace. This was why on the day of Pentecost, cloven tongues as of fire descended on each and every one of the disciples as the Holy Ghost filled them all (Acts 2:1-4)! After this episode, their

> The sent mentality that an apostle has should be complemented with a sense of urgency, always! This is crucial to note because most times, we mistake compliance for effectiveness.

apostolic capacity to reach out to all the nations of the world was activated.

> The Holy Ghost refreshes and enlivens us while the fire continually keeps our chambers ablaze for executing God's will promptly everywhere, even in the undulating, treacherous terrains of the marketplace.

6

BUILD WITH STONES AND NOT BRICKS

OUR UNIQUENESS IN CHRIST

For any God-given project and assignment to be acceptable to God, it must be carried out by God-given tools and resources. God is so immensely rich that He can supply every single believer with resources that can abundantly cater to all that they would ever ask or think. God does not have an assembly line in which He mass produces a mono-product. He runs a holy nation in which though everyone is powered by the same life that emanates from Him, they are nevertheless individually unique. This is so that no two believers are commissioned to carry out precisely the same assignment in the same way within the marketplace. He divinely works into each believer's unique frame the nuances and dimensional disparity of the assignment. The Bible declares,

> *You also, as LIVING STONES, are being built up a spiritual house, a holy priesthood, to offer up spiritual sacrifices acceptable to God through Jesus Christ* (1 Peter 2:5, NKJV).

God has the administrative resources to manage every believer's uniqueness in Christ. Consequently, the Bible refers to the believers as living stones. So, you see, God does not build with bricks but stones infused with and drenched in His life. I have seen houses built with stones – no two stones are the same! There is a unique dimension of Christ that is locked into each believer's vessel. Even though we are all of Christ, there is a unique manifestation that comes through each believer's life. So, God runs a decentralised system and builds with stones quarried by His Spirit.

> For any God-given project and assignment to be acceptable to God, it must be carried out by God-given tools and resources.

Satan however does not wield resources of infinite proportions. This means Satan does not have the administrative resources to manage people's uniqueness. Therefore, what he does is to group them together. Hence his use of bricks (which are characterised by definite, predictable dimensions) to build his bastion of iniquity in the world. Satan manages groups. He cannot manage individuals. This is what powers secular humanistic philosophy and diabolic social engineering.

For the apostle in the marketplace, there is always something unique that God commands them to do that is directly coupled to the inworking of God's grace within them.

After I got employed by the Federal Government of Nigeria, my colleagues and I were trained for two years. We were the pioneer staff so, the government spared no expense to equip us with all the knowledge and tools we would need to regulate the pricing of petroleum products. At the end of the training, we were honourably sent forth to become worthy ambassadors of the Nigerian government vis-à-vis the oil industry. This was a high point in our careers, and everyone was in high spirit. We were posted to different stations across the nation.

But no sooner did we hit the ground running than we realised that the reality on ground required something that was not even mentioned in our robust training modules - all our on-ground operations required integrity, but this was not remotely alluded to in any of our courses! Our course outlines touched on engineering, physics, mathematics, economics, accounting, etc. They did not by any means highlight integrity. Therefore, I had to rely on the operation of Christ within me to bring forth integrity and make righteousness the basis of all my dealings. And the more iniquity abounded in my office, the more the grace of God multiplied for me to represent Him in my sphere of the marketplace. In that season, my walk with God prospered many folds.

> That no two believers are commissioned to carry out precisely the same assignment in the same way within the marketplace.

BRICKS AND STONES IN THE HANDS OF MEN

Those who serve God build with stones. The Bible says,

The BRICKS have fallen down, But we will

rebuild with hewn STONES; (Isaiah 9:10, NKJV, emphasis added)

Those who serve themselves and the devil build with bricks. It would interest you to know that those who undertook the iniquitous project of building the Tower of Babel chose bricks over stones. The Bible says,

Then they said to one another, "Come, let us make bricks and bake them thoroughly." They had BRICK FOR STONE... (Genesis 11:3, NKJV, emphasis added)

Now, we have considered the fact that the believer is referred to as a living stone. Where are they hewn from? Here comes the answer:

"Listen to Me, you who follow after righteousness, You who seek the Lord: Look to the rock from which you were hewn, (Isaiah 51:1, NKJV)

For the avoidance of any doubt, the Lord is the rock of the believer's salvation (2 Samuel 22:47; Psalm 89:26). God is the source material from which the believer is hewn. God is also the source material from which the believer hews stones.

> Those who serve themselves and the devil build with bricks. It would interest you to know that those who undertook the iniquitous project of building the Tower of Babel chose bricks over stones.

So, what are stones in the hands of believers? Before we answer this question, let's look at the showdown between David and Goliath in the valley of Elah:

Then he took his staff in his hand; and he chose for himself FIVE SMOOTH STONES FROM THE BROOK, and PUT THEM IN A SHEPHERD'S BAG, IN A POUCH WHICH HE HAD, and his sling was in his hand. And he drew near to the Philistine.

Then David put his hand in his bag and took out a STONE; and he slung it and struck the Philistine in his forehead, so that the stone sank into his forehead, and he fell on his face to the earth.

So David prevailed over the Philistine with a sling and a STONE, and struck the Philistine and (1 Samuel 17:40, 49-50 NKJV, emphasis added)

> The 'stones' that the believer would use to slay the giant in their portion of the marketplace must be given to them by the Holy Spirit, who is the only one capable of reaching into the very depths of God to hew stones they can use in overcoming the world.

Note that from the above passage, stones were weapons in the hands of David. They were potent enough to slay a giant that terrorised his dear nation for weeks. How many stones did he pick? He picked five smooth stones. What does this mean? Five is the number of grace. The brook is a type of the Holy Spirit because the Holy Spirit is liquescent and can flow and be poured forth like water (Isaiah 32:15, Joel 2:28). Note also that the five stones were smooth because they had been in the brook long enough to be relieved of their rough edges.

Next, he put the stones in the pouch of his shepherd's bag. What does this mean? The stones were double hidden. The Bible says,

For you died, and YOUR LIFE IS HIDDEN WITH CHRIST IN GOD (Colossians 3:3, NKJV)

This all goes to show that the believer will achieve zero-result outside of Christ. The 'stones' that the believer would use to slay the giant in their portion of the marketplace must be given to them by the Holy Spirit, who is the only one capable of reaching into the very depths of God to hew stones they can use in overcoming the world.

Therefore, in simple terms, stones are Spirit-inspired ideas, concepts, solutions, deliverances etc., that can be used to solve knotty problems that seem to tower above all else in the believer's sphere of influence. Stones are equipment hewn from the righteous rock of God's eternal authority and power. These stones are life-based because they are released by the Holy Spirit to the believer as he or she seeks the Lord in communion. The believer conceives these *stones* during engagement with the Lord in deep, intimate fellowship. As the believer continues to take in these divine giant-killers, mystery solvers, *demon-rubbishers*, etc., they become pregnant with God's essence and receive His power and authority to bear the same in the marketplace. The truth is, whatever is born of God overcomes the world (1 John 5:4)!

So, in the context of this discourse, stones cannot be hewn from the brain and the soul; they are exclusively hewn from God by the Holy Spirit taking residence in the regenerated

BUILD WITH STONES AND NOT BRICKS

human spirit. Stones are strictly designed to build God's kingdom. This means apostles who wield them in the marketplace make the most of all opportunities given them to build out the kingdom of God among all people systems. To build out God's kingdom in the midst of any people system, giants must be slain, and we must uphold righteousness. And in keeping with Daniel's interpretation of Nebuchadnezzar's vision, God's kingdom is the giant piece of rock, hewn without human hands which smashes to pieces all the kingdoms of the world to make enough room for the kingdom of God to saturate the whole world. Every believer is a part of this giant rock of eternal glory and righteousness and unmatched strength!

In the same vein, bricks are demon-inspired concepts, ideas, innovations, and afflictions etc., which are used to lock down the four corners of the earth against the establishment of God's kingdom on earth. They are usually concocted by demons but released into the brains and souls of people for onward execution.

> **Stones cannot be hewn from the brain and the soul; they are exclusively hewn from God by the Holy Spirit taking residence in the regenerated human spirit.**

The scary thing about bricks is that they are not only wielded by unbelievers; they are also wielded by believers who wilfully fail to fully yield to the lordship of Jesus Christ. A believer who chooses not to remain fully submitted to the lordship of Christ at any point would soon become the quarry site of bricks. The devil always takes advantage of the slightest space created by the believer's refusal to completely bow to the majesty of Jesus Christ to pillage their soul. Look what the devil did to Judas' soul when Judas gave him a little space through avarice in his heart. See how ruthlessly the devil turned a one-time apostle of Jesus into a cold betrayer. If it were not for the

> Bricks are demon-inspired concepts, ideas, innovations, and afflictions etc., which are used to lock down the four corners of the earth against the establishment of God's kingdom on earth.

proactive prayer of Jesus, see how quickly Peter completely denied ever knowing Jesus in the heat of the moment. The only way to create no space for the devil is to yield all available space to Jesus Christ through unreserved submission to His lordship.

Whenever an apostle of the Lord Jesus Christ chooses brick over stone, they effectively start working for the devil.

> The devil always takes advantage of the slightest space created by the believer's refusal to completely bow to the majesty of Jesus Christ to pillage their soul.

GIFTS, MINISTRIES, AND OPERATIONS

Paul, in 1 Corinthians chapter 12, elaborately explains gifts, ministries, and operations. Let's briefly consider them as we trudge on in our discourse.

> *Now there are distinctive varieties and distributions of endowments (GIFTS, extraordinary powers distinguishing certain Christians, due to the power of divine grace operating in their souls by the Holy Spirit) and they vary, but the [Holy] Spirit remains the*

same. And there are distinctive varieties of service and MINISTRATION, but it is the same Lord [Who is served]. And there are distinctive varieties of OPERATION [of working to accomplish things], but it is the same God Who inspires and energizes them all in all. (1 Corinthians 12:4-6, AMP, emphasis added)

Gifts are special abilities conferred upon believers by the inworking of the Holy Spirit. They are released into the believers' chambers because of the willingness of the Spirit to dispense the excesses of God's bounties (Matthew 26:41). They are equipment given for the utilisation and expression of the power of God. The gifts are further discussed in 1 Corinthians 12:8-11.

Ministries are service platforms that are built in tandem with God's marching orders. When a believer receives instruction from God to carry out a specific task, He releases a unique consignment of grace for them to carry out the assignment. Obedience to God leads to the development of the consignment of grace, as a result of constant use and tireless application of themselves to it and by synergising with other believers. This goes on till the consignment of grace fructifies into a service platform where many people can subscribe and be blessed. Just as all the different parts of the body have distinct functions, so does every believer have a specific assignment from God to carry out. This is what ministry is about – whether it is within the body or in the marketplace. Ministries are further explained in 1 Corinthians 12: 12-27.

Operations are highly strategic platforms that God releases great grace upon faithful ministers to build in order to cater to territories. They are ministries whose structure and function are territorial in scope. Operations are run by men set by God within the body. Operations are concisely highlighted in 1 Corinthians 12:28-30.

Gifts, ministries, and operations have one common goal: the profit of all – not self-aggrandizement (1 Corinthians 12:7).

THE PARABLE OF WHEAT AND TARES

> *Another parable He put forth to them, saying: "The kingdom of heaven is like a man who sowed good seed in his field; but while men slept, his enemy came and sowed tares among the wheat and went his way. But when the grain had sprouted and produced a crop, then the tares also appeared. So the servants of the owner came and said to him, 'Sir, did you not sow good seed in your field? How then does it have tares?' He said to them, 'An enemy has done this.' The servants said to him, 'Do you want us then to go and gather them up?' But he said, 'No, lest while you gather up the tares you also uproot the wheat with them. Let both grow together until the harvest, and at the time of harvest I will say to the reapers, "First gather together the tares and bind them in bundles to burn them, but gather the wheat into my barn."'"* (Matthew 13:24-30, NKJV)

The parable above (known as the parable of the Wheat and Tares) is a continuation of the parable of the sower (Matthew 13:1-23). This is because the seeds that fell on the good ground blossom and flourish in different folds. When this happens, they are transplanted to the larger field of the world to grow with tares (wild, ungodly species). These are they who are likened to the good seeds in the parable of the sower. They are the ones in whom the word of God has prospered. The Lord harvests and transplants the seeds that fall on the good ground because they are loaded and buoyed by His government and authority to transmit and broadcast His kingdom and righteousness among the nations. The field is representative of platforms, systems, and social spaces. It is through these people that nations are healed. These are people planted in different sectors and spheres doing different things based on the unique operation of the Spirit of Christ on their inside to bring forth the corporate agenda of the kingdom of heaven on earth.

7

BETWEEN CAESAR AND GOD

Then the Pharisees went and consulted and plotted together how they might entangle Jesus in His talk. And they sent their disciples to Him along with the Herodians, saying, Teacher, we know that You are sincere and what You profess to be and that You teach the way of God truthfully, regardless of consequences and being afraid of no man; for You are impartial and do not regard either the person or the position of anyone. Tell us then what You think about this: Is it lawful to pay tribute [levied on individuals and to be paid yearly] to Caesar or not? But Jesus, aware of their malicious plot, asked, Why do you put Me to the test and try to entrap Me, you pretenders (hypocrites)? Show me the money used for the tribute. And they brought Him a denarius. And

Jesus said to them, Whose likeness and title are these? They said, Caesar's. Then He said to them, Pay therefore to Caesar the things that are due to Caesar, and pay to God the things that are due to God. (Matthew 22:15-21, AMP)

The passage above contains one of the occasions recorded in Scripture in which the Pharisees would weave a booby trap and tuck it in a seemingly simple question to entrap Jesus. This time, their sinister intention was to get Him to say something that would put Him in trouble with the Roman authorities. They had slyly prepared the noose. Any wrong answer from Him would have Him unwittingly put His neck in. But the supreme wisdom at work in Him saw right through them, and like other times, He would give them an answer that would not only stupefy them but would become a timeless jewel for generations on end.

At the time of this exchange between Jesus and the Pharisees, Rome was the world's superpower, and Caesar was its leader and the de facto leader of the world. Caesar was practically the face of the Roman Empire as he embodied its glory and splendour. His image and title were etched on everything Roman.

Rome had a very effective tax system in which every living soul within its colonies was required to pay an annual levy to the Roman authorities' coffers. In the days of Jesus' earthly ministry, Israel was one of the many Roman colonies, and each person was required to pay an annual levy as a tribute to Rome. The payment of the annual levy had been codified into law so that any refusal to pay was tantamount to treating the *almighty* Rome with ignominy.

However, Israel had been a direct or indirect theocracy for much of its existence. God ruled them Himself; and even when they began to have human kings, He ruled them indirectly through the kings because the kings had to take marching orders from the Lord through His prophets. Now, traditionally, an average Israelite knew that the Lord owned a portion of the work of their hands. So, it was normal practice in Israel for people to give to the Lord in the form of offerings.

> Work is spiritual. There's no such thing as secular work for the believer because secular means without God (atheos in the Greek). And those that are without God cannot do His work because they are estranged from Christ, alienated from the covenants of promise and the commonwealth of Israel, and utterly hopeless

When the Romans came along, they demanded a portion of the people's earnings in the form of taxes. The Roman tax system was designed to ensure efficiency in tax collection throughout all the colonies under Rome's control. To achieve efficiency, the Romans brilliantly came up with the idea of outsourcing tax collection to powerful locals who were required to remit certain fixed amounts to the Roman authorities. The amounts the tax collectors were to charge their people was completely at their discretion. This was very much to their advantage because anything else they generated outside the fixed amounts demanded by the Roman authorities was entirely theirs. This made tax collectors under the Roman system rich and chief tax collectors very wealthy!

Zacchaeus was a chief tax collector for the Roman Empire

in Israel. So being chief tax collector, he was at the pinnacle of his career and very rich too. He was so rich that when he met Jesus, he said he could afford to give half of his possessions to the poor, and if there was anybody he cheated, he would pay them four times over. However, tax collectors in those days were not exactly beloved because their business required being cold, merciless, underhanded, and cutthroat. The Jews were very nationalistic and loathed the occupation of Israel by Rome. They, therefore, saw tax collectors as renegade Jews who collaborated with foreign powers to lord it over their own people. Zacchaeus was not spared from the scourge of this sentiment. So, although he was wealthy, he was hated by his people. This was why when Jesus visited and consorted with Zacchaeus, it generated so much fuss and murmuring among some of the people (Luke 19:1-10).

> Wherever you are stationed in the marketplace, know that your number one instruction from the Lord is to serve those within the confinoo of your portion of the marketplace as though you were serving the Lord Himself.

Jesus' answer, however, cut through the angst and condensed frustration of the Israelites and the monolithic Roman occupation. It provided a paradigm that would serve as a template for practical apostolic work in the marketplace. He said simply: Give Caesar his due and give God His due. This reveals a strategy that creates a balance between God and Caesar. An apostle in the marketplace must always know how to strike a relationship balance between these two – we respectfully work with Caesar but worship God, with our number one priority being our worship to God. If at any point our contract with Caesar jeopardises our worship of God, Caesar should, by all means, be subordinated. Daniel and his comrades practically demonstrated this. Yes, always, we must give God His due and Caesar his due.

PRACTICAL RESOURCEFULNESS IN THE MARKETPLACE

Work is spiritual. There's no such thing as *secular work* for the believer because *secular* means *without God* (*atheos* in the Greek). And those that are without God cannot do His work because they are estranged from Christ, alienated from the covenants of promise and the commonwealth of Israel, and utterly hopeless (Ephesians 2:12). The work God gave Adam in the Garden of Eden was quotidian – it was far from spectacular. This is because he was required to manage and defend it, and in doing so, he would fulfil God's plan on earth.

You see, being an apostle of God in the marketplace means God has given you another kind of pulpit and audience. Your microphone and public address system would rather be the work of your hands. Your life, principles, and values would be your sermons, and the impact you make would be based on the effective exercise of your measure in Christ.

Many believers today see the marketplace of nations as the place where they make money and bring the money they have made into the church for the work of the ministry. They do not see their portion of the marketplace as a mission ground or a service platform for the work of the ministry. They call their work *secular* and not *ministry*. Well, the fact is, this is primarily due to the prevailing mentality of our day toward ministry, a mentality largely steeped in error. We are taught to consider any work not done within the four walls of the church as secular and work carried out within the four walls of the church as spiritual. But let us consider the following passages of Scripture together:

> *Whatever your hand finds to do, do it with your might; for there is no work or device or knowledge or wisdom in the grave where you are going.* (Ecclesiastes 9:10, NKJV)

> *Bondservants, be obedient to those who are your masters according to the flesh, with fear and trembling, in sincerity of heart, as to Christ; not with eyeservice, as men-pleasers, but as bondservants of Christ, doing the will of God from the heart, with goodwill doing service, as to the Lord, and not to men, knowing that whatever good anyone does, he will receive the same from the Lord, whether he is a slave or free.* (Ephesians 6:5-8, NKJV)

> *Bondservants, obey in all things your masters according to the flesh, not with eyeservice, as men-pleasers, but in sincerity of heart, fearing God. And whatever you do, do it heartily, as to the Lord and not to men, knowing that from the Lord you will receive the reward of the inheritance; for you serve the Lord Christ. But he who does wrong will be repaid for what he has*

done, and there is no partiality. (Colossians 3:22-25, NKJV)

The first quotation is an admonition from the wise king Solomon. The following two passages are admonitions given by Paul to both the Ephesian and Colossian churches. The common denominator in all three quotations is WORK! Solomon's warning is pretty straightforward. Paul's rebuke is also straightforward but with a little twist. The little twist is that in Paul's day, slavery was still universally condoned. There were some slaves who had accepted the lordship of Jesus Christ. They seemed to have two masters – their human masters and the Lord Jesus Christ! Now, by the apostolic wisdom operational in Paul's life and ministry, he gave the Christian slaves a pragmatic counsel received straight from God's heart. Being an occasional entrepreneur himself, Paul knew the importance of work and admonished the Christian slaves to work for their human masters as though they were working for God. He did not stop there. He said the Lord Himself would reward them for serving their human masters wholeheartedly!

> You see, there is no such thing as full-time or part-time ministry; there is just the ministry. These inaccurate labels of full-time and part-time ministry are man-made, unfounded in Scriptures, and meant to erroneously create an imaginary dichotomy between ministry within the church and in the marketplace.

So, no, the marketplace is not just for making money and extracting money to bring into the church (which in itself is not bad). It is a place for harvesting souls for the Lord that would never otherwise make it to the four walls of the church. Remember that Philip was practically sent to intercept the Ethiopian eunuch *on the road* (not in the temple in Jerusalem) for the eunuch to be harvested into the kingdom. The emphasis was the salvation of the Ethiopian eunuch's soul and his acceptance of the lordship of Jesus Christ and not the fact that he was in charge of Ethiopia's entire treasury. Remember also that the fields are white and ready for harvest *in the world* and not *in the church*. The church is a depot of sorts designed for training and releasing apostles into the marketplace of the nations (Ephesians 4:11-12).

Again, I say work is spiritual! Are you an entrepreneur, employee or employer, athlete, artisan, trader, or entertainer? Do you have to wake up and show up at work or your place of business daily, weekly, fortnightly, and monthly? Wherever you are stationed in the marketplace, know that your number one instruction from the Lord is to serve those within the confines of your portion of the marketplace as though you were serving the Lord Himself. Always strike a balance between Caesar and God. You cannot allow your work to suffer for any reason. And if you are like me and you have to serve the Lord intensively within the body of Christ, and in the marketplace, God will supply ample grace to give you sufficient capacity to handle both. Ministry is serving God by serving people.

If you are a banker, your portion of the marketplace is the banking sector. Except the Lord instructs you otherwise, your ministry is the banking space. And except the Lord instructs you otherwise (which is usually a big exception), you do not have *to* resign from the banking job to go into ministry full time. You see, there is no such thing as full-time or part-time ministry; there is just the ministry. These inaccurate labels of *full-time* and *part-time* ministry are man-made, unfounded in Scriptures, and meant to erroneously create an imaginary dichotomy between ministry within the church and in the marketplace. Are you a barber, hairstylist, classroom teacher, etc.? Do it wholeheartedly as unto the Lord. Your true reward is not the salaries or the monetary gains you get for creating value; your true reward will come from the Lord.

There is not supposed to be any dichotomy between those who serve the Lord within the church and those who serve the Lord within the marketplace. The synergy between these God's servants would bring the fullness of Christ on earth and unleash His light in the world. This is clearly illustrated by the following passage:

> **The Amalekites came and attacked the Israelites at Rephidim. Moses said to Joshua, "Choose some of our men and go out to fight the Amalekites. Tomorrow I will stand on top of the hill with the staff of God in my hands." So Joshua fought the Amalekites as Moses had ordered, and Moses, Aaron, and Hur went to the top of the hill. As long as Moses held up his hands, the Israelites were winning, but whenever he lowered his hands, the Amalekites were winning. When Moses' hands grew tired, they took a stone and put it under him and he sat**

> on it. Aaron and Hur held his hands up — one on one side, one on the other — so that his hands remained steady till sunset. So Joshua overcame the Amalekite army with the sword. (Exodus 17:8-13, NIV)

> **The staff of God in Moses' hands was not really needed on the field. And Joshua's sword was useless on the hilltop. But when the two were made to synergistically leverage each other.**

I would like us to briefly observe the synergy between the staff of God in Moses' hands on the hilltop and the sword of Joshua in the field. Note that Moses did not go to the top of the hill alone; neither did Joshua go to the battlefield alone. Moses had a team with him (Aaron and Hur), while Joshua had some warriors with him. So, we see two teams here; one on the hill and the other on the field. Elsewhere I called this the *Hill-Field Strategy*.

For the conquest of the Amalekites to become a reality, Moses' and Joshua's teams had to pool all resources together synergistically and leverage each other's strengths to ensure everyone did their bit. Moses was God's set man on the hilltop; Joshua was God's point man on the battle-field. Aaron and Hur and the warriors under Joshua's command were the much-needed support system that quietly laboured to ensure that the victory against the Amalekites was sure and total. I dare say that without Aaron, Hur, and Joshua's warriors, there would not have been a victory recorded for Israel against the Amalekites on that day – Moses and Joshua would not have clinched victory without working with their teams.

The staff of God in Moses' hands was not really needed on the field. And Joshua's sword was useless on the hilltop. But when the two were made to synergistically leverage each other, the result was the comprehensive defeat of the Amalekites. This is very instructive.

THE SERPENT-DOVE IMPACT MODEL

There is no walk of life, people system, or sphere of influence that is a no-go area. In these last days, God is sending apostles to every inch and square foot of the marketplace. The Holy Ghost is the Spirit of the age to come; therefore, He is eternally ahead of the curve of human civilisation. His relevance with man is for all eternity. No trend or fad can catch Him off guard or take Him unawares.

The world is a jungle. It is an aberration and mutation in progress. It is a wild – littered with foul creatures that bear and broadcast darkness. It is not designed to be kind to the average believer. It is specially built to have steely antipathy toward the Christian faith. Our Lord and Master Jesus has warned us already about the world's default belligerence toward God's cause on earth and anyone who dares to promote it. He has given us an impact strategy that would help us to not only cope with the world's hostilities but to prosper in carrying out God's will in the marketplace of the nations. He said,

> ***Behold, I am sending you out like sheep in the midst of wolves; be wary and wise as serpents,***

and be innocent (harmless, guileless, and without falsity) as doves (Matthew 10:16, AMP)

Ordinarily, sheep do not stand a chance amidst wolves. But Jesus says they do: If they adopt what I call the Serpent-Dove Impact Model in the apostolic conquest of the marketplace of the nations. To fully grasp this, we need to briefly consider the animals mentioned in the verse of Scripture above and the relationship among them.

Concerning sheep and wolves, Jesus said,

> *Beware of false prophets, who come to you dressed as* SHEEP, *but inside they are* DEVOURING WOLVES (Matthew 7:15, AMP)

> Why then would Jesus charge believers to adopt the ways of the serpent in their apostolic work in the marketplace? The reason is that they are highly strategic. They move with great finesse and tact and strike with great precision and speed. They embody the pragmatic, on-ground ability to adapt and adopt.

Note the adjective *devouring* that is used to describe wolves. It goes to fully explain what wolves are about: a gaping, wild appetite. This makes wolves essentially frenetic. Wolves are ravening because they are almost always driven by their hunger for prey. Their formation, community, and entire lives are an evolution of their need to satisfy their ever-seething, acrimonious hunger. Their appetite is their lord. Their loyalty is to no one else but their self-serving hunger.

Sheep are known to have the capacity to be both loyal and

obedient to an entity apart from themselves. They have the ability to rely on someone other than themselves to sort everything about their lives – therefore, they have shepherds.

Serpents are known to be cunning, crafty, and devious. They are essentially wily. The devil himself is metaphorically referred to as the old serpent (Revelation 20:2). Why then would Jesus charge believers to adopt the ways of the serpent in their apostolic work in the marketplace? The reason is that they are highly strategic. They move with great finesse and tact and strike with great precision and speed. They embody the pragmatic, on-ground ability to adapt and adopt. Note that Jesus made a comparison between Himself and a serpent thus,

> **And as Moses lifted up the serpent in the wilderness, even so must the Son of man be lifted up** (John 3:14, KJV)

Doves epitomise harmlessness. One prominent feature of the dove's anatomy is that it does not have a gallbladder. Quite interesting isn't it? The primary function of the gallbladder is to store and concentrate bile (an acrid enzyme) needed for the digestion of food. The dove does not have a gallbladder. What does this mean? Symbolically, it means the dove is incapable of either storing up bitterness or being bitter itself.

So putting all these together, we can surmise the following: The Lord is our shepherd, and we are the sheep of His pasture, as we go into the marketplace of nations and interface with people driven by rapacious desires, ravening ambitions, and avarice (as propelled and compelled by very belligerent spirits).

We must rely on the wisdom and power of God to be underwhelmed by the litany of challenges that will come as we adapt and adopt Holy Ghost-spawned strategies and be incapable of paying back evil for evil because once and again, we shall be pierced through with javelins of offences, betrayals, and inconveniences. Our perfect example in all this is Jesus, who was fully led by God, wielded God's unmatchable wisdom and power, and passed up on all the opportunities He got to unleash incalculable pain on those who hurt Him. Even in His most excruciating moment on the cross, He chose to forgive those who drove Roman iron spikes through His body to plague Him with sanity-shredding pain.

I cannot tell you how many times I have been cheated in business; and sometimes by brethren in Christ. How many times things were going downhill, and I faced the temptation to abandon God's instructions and leadership and do my own thing. And, how many times I almost had a nervous breakdown because circumstances were becoming seemingly too overwhelming to bear. But through it all, the Lord, my shepherd, came through for me and swallowed my troubles whole! You see, whenever we go through situations that are way beyond our capacity to bear, it is not God being untrue and unfaithful. It is Him bringing us to the end of ourselves so that we would trust in no one else, not even ourselves, but Him alone! Paul said,

> **For we do not want you to be ignorant, brethren, of our trouble which came to us in Asia: that we were burdened beyond measure, above strength, so that we despaired even of life. Yes, we had the sentence of death in ourselves, that we should not trust in ourselves but in God who raises the dead** (2 Corinthians 1:8-9, NKJV)

The world system is more than space, time, and matter. It is also much more than people and geography. The world system is a thoroughly organised system specially tempered, formulated, and forged to squelch and extinguish God on earth. It is the most comprehensive and organised rebellion against the kingdom of God and His righteousness. Interfacing with the world system is being in a war zone.

The Bible says,

> **No one engaged in warfare entangles himself with the affairs of this life.** (2 Timothy 2:4, NKJV)

What are some of the affairs of this life? They are the multidimensional multi-faceted, soul-numbing cares of this world and deceitfulness of riches (Matthew 13:22).

The ruthless enemy of our souls has his minions constantly working overtime to ensure every single believer is bombarded with these. The machines and mortars of hell are stationed in every inch of the world system to ensure the believer is constantly distracted from consistently engaging the two most important pillars of the Christian faith system, namely:

1. The ministry of the word
2. Prayer

(Acts 6:4)

The supernatural victory that is supposed to be a Christian's daily experience is hinged upon these two pillars.

> Whenever we go through situations that are way beyond our capacity to bear, it is not God being untrue and unfaithful. It is God bringing us to the end of ourselves so that we would trust in no one else, not even ourselves, but Him alone!

Sadly, many Christians today do not give themselves continually to prayer and the ministry of the word. Little wonder that the power surge meant to rise from believers' lives on account of the latent power of the Holy Ghost in them to bring down satanic installations in their spheres of influence is reduced to deplorable levels!

I have stated elsewhere that one of the weapons a country must have to qualify as a military superpower in the twenty-first century is the aircraft carrier capable of unleashing Armageddon wherever it is pitched. The United States has 20 commissioned aircraft carriers, whereas China has only one! It is for this reason that to date, no nation comes close to the superior military might of the United States of America.

But one million aircraft carriers cannot deal with the least demon from hell. Because, aircraft carriers are man-made, carnal weapons.

Therefore, the Holy Ghost in the believer is mightier than any man-made weaponry. He can empower the believer to destroy every work of darkness, trample underfoot any devil that dares try them. Yet many believers do not take advantage of His residence in them.

There is too much distraction for children of God these days. Bills, bills, and more bills are the excuses for the power outage in the lives of many believers.

Every believer has received tremendous power on account of receiving the Holy Ghost (Acts 1:8). This power is latent,

> You can't engage the Holy Ghost on this level and be depressed or need UEFA Champions League or the next box office hit to drive away boredom or escape sorrow.

unexploited like crude oil. There are well over one thousand products that can be extracted from crude oil. To get these products, the crude has to be subjected to different temperatures through heating. In other words, no heat, no product!

How much of the 'crude' deposit of the Holy Ghost we exploit and maximise is not up to God. No! It is entirely up to us.

Power has been made available to all believers, but not all believers are powerful. Why? Heat!

I lived and worked in Lagos (which is unarguably the busiest city in Nigeria) for close to six years, during which the devil tried every possible trick in his bag to shut down my prayer life and truncate my engagement with the ministry of the word. It was crazy I tell you. I had to learn to study the Bible amid migraine-dishing generator noise. I converted the long hours I spent in traffic during my commute to and from work to heat the 'crude reserves' in the chambers of my spirit – by praying in the spirit always. The delivery of the Holy Ghost power products did not stop as I basked in the endless refreshing of God's presence. I enjoyed power surge nonstop. The devil failed! Hallelujah!

If you continually heat up the crude reserves by prayer and study, the power surge would cause you to explode endlessly with Holy Ghost power products. You can't engage the Holy Ghost on this level and be depressed or need UEFA Champions League or the next box office hit to drive away boredom or escape sorrow.

You would not need any external stimulant to spice up your life. You would experience firsthand the kingdom of God, which is what the Bible says is not meat and drink (external merriment, euphoria, and conviviality) but righteousness, peace, and joy in the Holy Ghost! (Romans 14:17)

There is no excuse to be powerless, cold, and depressed, my friend. Engage the Holy Ghost in you and keep the products coming. A cold stove is no threat to cockroaches. So, heat up!

8

GRACE AND DILIGENCE

For I am the least of the apostles and do not even deserve to be called an apostle, because I persecuted the church of God. But by the grace of God I am what I am, and His grace to me was not without effect. No, I worked harder than all of them — yet not I, but the grace of God that was with me (1 Corinthians 15:9-10, NIV)

Grace is the ecosystem that supports all kingdom operations - like water is to aquatic life. It is the only valid environment in which all faith-based activities can occur. I have written elsewhere that grace is the central feature that most incontestably separates the Christian faith system from all other religions under the heaven. No other faith system on earth has grace at its operational and constitutional core. Christ embodies and personifies grace. So being in Christ opens a believer up to all the potentials of grace.

Grace is at the centre of our faith system and defines the circumference of the Christian life and experience. From salvation (which is the entry-level experience of the Christian); through the transformation of the soul to the climactic glorification of the believer, grace makes it all happen.

In Christian service, grace makes available the limitless abilities of God and the incorruptibility of His divine life for the believer's advantage. One of the major ways grace operates is to superimpose God's infinitude upon human limitations so that the believer can do the supernatural naturally, and the natural supernaturally! The grace of God covers the quotidian as well as the spectacular aspects of the Christian journey of faith. And as we shall soon see, one of the ways the grace of God is made most manifest is through work. Because, in the beginning, God worked. God rested from His creation and commissioned man so that man would continue to do God's work.

> **Grace is the ecosystem that supports all kingdom operations - like water is to aquatic life.**

By human categorisation and classification, Paul was indeed the least of the apostles because he joined the fold after Jesus had physically left the earth and had the most unworthy past of them all. But the grace of God transformed him into an apostle of the Lord Jesus Christ. And the most distinctive way in which the grace of God operated in his life was to supernaturally enable him to work the hardest of all the apostles. In his own words, he worked harder than all the apostles. He was unarguably the most prolific of all the apostles. He penned approximately fifty percent of the New Testament. The operation of the grace of God in his life made his output far outweigh that of the other apostles. And he categorically

> One of the major ways grace operates is to superimpose God's infinitude upon human limitations so that the believer can do the supernatural naturally, and the natural supernaturally!

states in the passage of Scripture quoted above that his excellent work had nothing to do with him but everything to do with the grace of God.

Here, you can see that the proof that Paul had a robust supply of God's grace was in how hard he worked. His work was the fruit of the torrential release of God's grace. The seismic impact his ministry had in the Gentile world was a further testament to how much work he put in the gospel of the Lord Jesus Christ.

Now the labour Paul exerted and the energy he expended in his apostolic ministry to the Gentiles did not come from him; it came from God in the form of grace. There was no way Paul would have done all he did on the battery of human strength and discipline. The multitude of sufferings and ordeals that were slammed on him by the dark forces in the Gentile world on account of his devotion to Christ were enough to make him snap and give up. His human strength had been overwhelmed many times, but the grace of God in his life was intensified once and again to keep him going. And in his words, the grace of God was not made to be without effect in his life. He deliberately engaged the grace of God to achieve maximum results.

Therefore, my emphasis is on the fact that Paul engaged the grace of God to maximise apostolic productivity. He did not waste the grace of God through apathy – he placed maximum demand on the grace of God throughout his time with the Lord on this side of eternity.

> **Paul engaged the grace of God to maximise apostolic productivity. He did not waste the grace of God through apathy - he placed maximum demand on the grace of God throughout his time with the Lord on this side of eternity.**

THE DANGER OF GRACE IN INERTIA

There is a dangerous wave of teachings currently being peddled in some parts of the body of Christ that espouses that grace does not need work to fructify. The proponents of this copiously quote Ephesians 2:8-9 to support this fractured doctrinal stance thus:

> *For by grace are ye saved through faith; and that not of yourselves: it is the gift of God: Not of works, lest any man should boast* (Ephesians 2:8-9, KJV)

Salvation is a gift that is accessible by believing in the Lord Jesus Christ. What makes this possible is the grace of God embodied by Jesus Christ that can be touched through faith. It requires zero human labour to be appropriated. True. But those who say grace is not associated with work of any kind do not know that there are kinds of works:

1. Dead works (Hebrews 6:1; 9:14)
These are works that are executed by the man who is yet to be quickened by the Spirit of the Lord – who is yet to accept the grace of God that leads to salvation, through faith, and be saved.

2. Good works (Ephesians 2:10)
They are called good works because they hail from God resident within the vessel of a believer (a person who has been saved by grace through faith). Note good works are *good* not because they are benevolent and beneficial but because their origin is God. Therefore, a person who is not saved cannot do good works, period!

The next verse that follows the verses quoted above clearly states:

> *For we are his workmanship,* **CREATED IN CHRIST JESUS UNTO GOOD WORKS,** *which God hath before ordained that we should walk in them.* (Ephesians 2:10, KJV, emphasis mine)

This means the reason why a believer is saved is not for them alone – God has a purpose for salvation – it is called good works. Which is why after salvation has been worked into the believer, they are required to work it out so that others can benefit from the same. This is in keeping with God's eternal benevolence (Philippians 2:12-13). Jesus said,

> It is not enough to receive grace. We have to learn to extend the same to others. This is best achieved through service.

Let your light so shine before men, that they

may see your GOOD WORKS and glorify your Father in heaven. (Matthew 5:16, NKJV, emphasis mine)

So you see, it takes good works executed by believers for men to glorify God in heaven.

> **To refuse to carry out good works is to make the grace of God of no effect.**

It is not enough to receive grace. We have to learn to extend the same to others. This is best achieved through service. Therefore, ministry is about sharing the grace that God has given us with others. If we have been blessed to have received grace, we must learn to extend the same to others through good works.

One of the first things God said to Abraham was,

> *"I will make you into a great nation and I will bless you; I will make your name great, and you will be a blessing."* (Gen 12:2, NIV)

It is clear from God's word to Abraham that the reason why He would bless Abraham was not for him alone. It was so that Abraham could become a channel of blessing to others. Every recipient of grace has been equally blessed by God, as affirmed by Paul when He said,

> *'Praise be to the God and Father of our Lord Jesus Christ, who has blessed us in the heavenly realms with every spiritual blessing in Christ.'* (Eph 1:3-4, NIV).

Being so blessed by God is not only a great privilege but equally a great responsibility. God frowns at the hoarding of grace.

All recipients of grace must learn to become channels of grace for others to enjoy. God does not call people to enjoy grace alone. He calls people to both enjoy and extend grace to others. It is, therefore, wicked to enjoy grace alone without bestowing it to others. Grace can only be extended to others through good works. This requires using the grace of God as fuel to do great and mighty things in His name.

Consequently, to refuse to carry out good works is to make the grace of God of no effect. Like the servant who was given one talent and refused to trade with it but rather elected to dig a hole and bury it – put it in a state of inertia. This was how he ended,

> **He who had received one talent also came forward, saying, Master, I knew you to be a harsh and hard man, reaping where you did not sow, and gathering where you had not winnowed [the grain]. So I was afraid, and I went and hid your talent in the ground. Here you have what is your own. But his master answered him, YOU WICKED AND LAZY AND IDLE SERVANT! Did you indeed know that I reap where I have not sowed and gather [grain] where I have not winnowed? Then you should have invested my money with the bankers, and at my coming I would have received what was my own with interest. So take the talent away from him and**

give it to the one who has the ten talents. For to everyone who has will more be given, and he will be furnished richly so that he will have an abundance; but from the one who does not have, even what he does have will be taken away. AND THROW THE GOOD-FOR-NOTHING SERVANT INTO THE OUTER DARKNESS; THERE WILL BE WEEPING AND GRINDING OF TEETH. (Matthew 25:24-30, AMP, emphasis mine)

So, you see, to not productively engage the grace of God by producing good works is tantamount to being wicked and lazy. It takes extreme wickedness and laziness to refuse to put the grace of God to work. Putting the grace of God that we have received into a state of inertia has disastrous consequences of eternal proportions – it shall attract serious punishment on the other side of eternity. The good-for-nothing servant was cast into outer darkness to be severely punished. Note he was a servant (therefore was born again, saved) who refused to develop the grace of God in his life into a service platform for others to benefit from the grace that he had received. He did not execute good works therefore he was good-for-nothing!

> **To not productively engage the grace of God by producing good works is tantamount to being wicked and lazy**

DILIGENCE: THE KEY TO DEALING WITH THE SEEDS AND FRUITS OF WICKEDNESS AND LAZINESS

The word *wicked* comes from the Old English *Wicca*, which is wizard, witch, and by extension, witchcraft and wizardry. You might be wondering what this has got to do with laziness. Everything! Now, if God commands a believer to carry out an assignment and they do not, we call this rebellion. Rebellion is simply the refusal to carry out God's will, whether actively or passively. Active rebellion is deliberately going in a totally different direction from the one contained in God's instruction, like Jonah. While passive rebellion is simply being lazy – not taking the initiative and responsibility; not giving it all it takes to carry out God's instruction – just standing aloof and hoping that things would get themselves done somehow. Because of laziness, those who are supposed to rise on their feet and clinch their ordination of being gods shall die like mere men (Psalms 82:6-7)

The Bible directly links rebellion and witchcraft in this verse of Scripture below:

> **For rebellion is as the sin of witchcraft...**
> (1 Samuel 15:23, NKJV)

We cannot bring profit to God if we do not productively engage His grace in our lives. We do not work to be saved, but we are saved to work. If we allow the grace of God that we have received in us to lay dormant, we and our generation are bound to suffer

> Let's face it, as a servant of God, especially in the marketplace; you must fan the embers of diligence daily into a conflagration of productivity in your life.

torment.

Let's face it, as a servant of God, especially in the marketplace; you must fan the embers of diligence daily into a conflagration of productivity in your life. You must put in the hours, press past the pain and draw upon the grace of God to build stamina and staying power. In whatever part of the marketplace you are, you must give your best! I have had to acquire skills, build disciplines and commit extra time to receive training that would put me on the cutting edge at my office. Countless times, I would move straight from rigorously intensive crusades and conferences to the office. I would travel by road, air, and sometimes even on boats to fulfil my apostolic mandate to the body of Christ. Then move straight back to my day job to fulfil my apostolic mandate in the marketplace. Sometimes my health would be strained, to breaking point - running stomachs, fevers, body aches, sleep deprivation among other things. But I would cry to the Lord for mercy, and He always answered me.

> For in the marketplace of nations, what gives you an audience with the kings are the tangible, valuable and practicable solutions that are the by-products of the works of your hands.

As you rise higher in your obedience to the heavenly vision, most of the time, you would have to connect to the superior mechanics and operations of God's grace that have nothing to do with nerve endings. This implies that you would practically be taught by the Holy Spirit how to walk in covenant, which is far higher than walking by what you feel or think. For sometimes you would not even feel like staying on course, but when heaven's duty calls, you must obey. In good times and bad times, in triumphs and setbacks, in heavy gains and losses, on crests and in troughs: by covenant, you override the dictates of your senses, environment, flesh, and the devil – to connect to a higher power source that cannot be depleted. This is called the tenacity of covenant living.

Show up, clock in, let the wisdom of God on your inside churn out incredible solutions in your place of work or business. Let the power of God at work in you grind to mush everything that resists the extension of the frontiers of God's kingdom. Productivity runs on the four tyres of diligence.

For three years I was persecuted by a top echelon executive in my organisation. He ensured I was not promoted for those three years. I sought the Lord's face on the matter, and found comfort in Him. I did not stop discharging my duties to the best of my God-given abilities. After three years, I got working with a new boss who was quite impressed by my dedication and quality of work. The Lord stirred his heart in my favour and he decided to have a look at my file. While perusing my file, he noticed I had not been promoted for three years and, upon thorough investigation, found out I had done nothing to deserve such cruelty. He took my issue on and wrote a petition to the headquarters for a speedy resolution of my case. I was promoted. My promotion was backdated to three years with full benefits of the three years paid. And, yes, it dawned on me that what seemed to be persecution was really the government helping me save for three years. So, I built my first house on government savings! Meanwhile, the man who persecuted me later got sacked for some convoluted reasons.

It breaks my heart each time I see Christians take their work lightly. The proof that you are spiritually healthy is how productive you are. By being productive, I mean all round productivity – in your Christian life as well as the works of your hands. For in the marketplace of nations, what gives you an audience with the kings are the tangible, valuable and practicable solutions that are the by-products of the works of your hands. Simply put, they would not hear the gospel you have to preach without first knowing what you can do.

MEASURES IN CHRIST

I stated earlier that God has the administrative resources to cater to everyone's uniqueness in Christ. Throughout Scriptures (both Testaments), God's making of man is directly and metaphorically represented as a one-on-one encounter or act. God is very hands-on with His creation. For instance, in Jeremiah 18:1-6, God is referred to as the Potter. Pottery is an art and craft that requires working directly with the hands. A potter's workshop is not an assembly line. It is a platform for unique creations. So, every piece in the potter's workshop was made from the potter's personal creative might and exertion.

In the new creation, God is directly involved with the making (recreating) of everyone in Christ. In His eternal wisdom, He has deemed it necessary not to create a machine by which He can mass produce. This is because everyone matters to Him, and no one is an ecumenical statistic. He gives infinite attention to anyone who is alive in Him by faith and personally transforms all those who yield to His government. Such is the eternal efficacy of God's economy – everyone is thoroughly captured in the budget that is drawn from His eternal riches and Godhead. Therefore, the Bible says,

> *For we are God's [own] handiwork (His workmanship), recreated in Christ Jesus* (Ephesians 2:10, AMP)

Consequently, Christ is the workshop in which every believer is recreated. This is why every believer has a life allocation called *measure* by which they live, move, and have their being. Paul elaborately covered the measure of the believer's faith in Christ: a proper understanding of which will kill competition and spur collaboration and synergy among believers.

The Pauline epistles are replete with the subject matter of the believer's measure in Christ. Paul thunders this in Romans 12:3; 2 Corinthians 10: 13-15, 11:23, 12:7; and Ephesians 4:7, 13, and 16.

> **Everyone is thoroughly captured in the budget that is drawn from His eternal riches and Godhead.**

The word measure in Greek is *metron* (from which the English word metre is derived) and *kanon* (from which the English word canon is derived). Meter (a standard portion, unit of measurement) and canon (a standard, boundary). These two words suggest operational capacity with a defined boundary. This further suggests that the uniqueness of every believer in Christ is defined by their operational capacity and boundary; suggesting completeness and limitation at the same time. This means that although complete in Christ, every believer is still operationally limited by design - yes, God's own design. So that the body of Christ can only achieve its full potential if individually complete members recognise their need for other members, thereby encouraging synergy and interdependence.

It is worthy of note that only God is complete in Himself and operationally complete, needing no external help to excel. He is all-powerful, with zero weakness!

It is imperative to understand one's measure in Christ because it lets them know what they can contribute to others and why they need others - their strengths and weaknesses. Humility is essentially operating within one's measure in Christ. Pride is working outside of one's measure in Christ. This is more so true because when one operates

> Christ is the workshop in which every believer is recreated. This is why every believer has a life allocation called measure by which they live, move, and have their being.

within their measure in Christ, they exalt Christ. Whereas when one operates outside their measure in Christ, they project themselves. For the apostle of the Lord Jesus Christ, they must learn the full dimensions of what is available to them in Christ. One big temptation is always trying to prove a point by operating outside one's measure in Christ. This is very serious and dangerous.

Paul said,

> *And to keep me from being puffed up and too much elated by the exceeding greatness (preeminence) of these revelations, there was given me a thorn (a splinter) in the flesh, a messenger of Satan, to rack and buffet and harass me, to keep me from being excessively exalted. Three times I called upon the Lord and besought [Him] about this and begged that it might depart from me; But He said to me, My grace (My favor and loving-kindness and mercy) is enough for you [sufficient against any danger and enables you to bear the trouble manfully]; for My strength and power are made perfect (fulfilled and completed) and show themselves most effective in [your] weakness. Therefore, I will all the more gladly glory in my weaknesses and infirmities, that the strength and power of Christ (the Messiah) may rest (yes, may pitch a tent over and dwell) upon me!*
> (2 Corinthians 12:7-9, AMP)

It is simple:

- Do not go beyond what God has given you the grace to do.
- God only gives grace to support that which He has commanded
- Do not pre-empt God.
- When in doubt, pray, pray, and pray until the answer comes. Sometimes the answers come from the ministry of other believers.

> Although complete in Christ, every believer is still operationally limited by design - yes, God's own design. So that the body of Christ can only achieve its full potential if individually complete members recognise their need for other members, thereby encouraging synergy and interdependence

- Grace does not make it easy; it makes it doable.
- For those heavily endowed by God, He will go to any length to keep them humble.
- God only blesses and rewards works done within the confines of the believer's measure in Christ. Whatever is done outside the believer's measure in Christ is null and void.

9

THE LORD'S CUP AND THE CUP OF DEVILS

You cannot drink the cup of the Lord and the cup of demons; you cannot partake of the Lord's Table and of the table of demons. (1 Corinthians 10:21, NKJV)

The solemnity of the passage above deserves deep mediation as it can elude a casual consideration. Two sets of items are listed side by side:

1. The cup of the Lord and the cup of demons
2. The Lord's Table and the table of demons

Note that it is not the Lord's cup and the devil's cup. Also, it is not the Lord's Table and the devil's table. It is the Lord's cup and demons' cup; and the Lord's Table and the table of demons. It is One Lord, one cup versus many demons, one cup. It is One Lord, one table versus many demons, one table. It is practically the Lord versus demons! Why? Because, like I said in the preceding chapter, only God is complete within Himself and by Himself and needs no external help to excel. God is uncreated – He exists of His own accord through the boundless stretches of eternity while the devil was created. God is operationally unlimited, while the devil is operationally limited. God is omnipotent and omnipresent, while the devil is not. So how does the devil broadcast his quasi-presence throughout the four corners of the world? He does this by a well organised demonic horde across nearly every people system on earth.

> God is uncreated - He exists of His own accord through the boundless stretches of eternity while the devil was created. God is operationally unlimited, while the devil is operationally limited. God is omnipotent and omnipresent, while the devil is not.

Therefore, whereas the Lord always acts as One Lord through One Spirit (Ephesians 4:4-5), the devil always acts as one being through many spirits. This is adumbrated by the one rod-serpent of Aaron (powered by the Lord) that was taken on by the many rod-serpents of the Egyptian sorcerers (powered by demons) (Exodus 7:10-12).

In light of the above explanation, let us now move into understanding the implication of these two sets of items.

THE LORD'S CUP

> *Then He said to them, "My soul is exceedingly sorrowful, even to death. Stay here and watch with Me." He went a little farther and fell on His face, and prayed, saying, "O My Father, if*

it is possible, let this cup pass from Me; nevertheless, not as I will, but as You will." (Matthew 26:38-39, NKJV)

Note that Jesus said *His soul was sorrowful even unto death* –He could feel the cold hands of death pawing over the membrane of His soul. The thirst in His soul had reached its climax. His first and only viable option was to quench the arcane thirst in His soul with the drink in the Lord's cup. The content of the Lord's cup would bind His soul in covenant with God down the inglorious valley of incalculable pain. He had discerned that the Lord's cup was the Lord's will for Him. The Lord's cup was the requisite suffering for the completion of His redemptive work on earth. The content of the Lord's cup could only be drunk by His soul.

So, the Lord's cup is the Lord's will that is figured in requisite suffering. The Lord's cup is only drunk by souls that are ready to be bound in covenant with God to execute His will no matter the cost, even to the death.

THE CUP OF DEMONS

The cup of demons is antithetical to the Lord's cup in that they exalt self-seeking, self-preserving, and self-sustaining alternatives above the will of God. The cup of demons is the compromise that binds the soul in covenant with demons.

THE LORD'S TABLE

The Lord's Table is where Lord's food is served and eaten. This is the exclusive preserve of those who are shepherded by Him.

Those who God shepherds have their souls restored by Him, and He faithfully sticks with them as they make their journey through the valley of the shadow of death as a consequence of drinking of His cup. These and much more they enjoy (Psalms 23:1-6).

The Lord's Table has only one menu. This menu is revealed by Jesus Himself thus,

> **"MY FOOD IS TO DO THE WILL OF HIM WHO SENT ME, AND TO FINISH HIS WORK"** (John 4:34, NKJV, emphasis added)

The Lord's food is doing the will of He who has sent us and to finish His work. For our context, this simply means carrying out His apostolic mandate to the letter. This inextricably connects doing God's will with work – good works of course. The soul of an apostle of God in the marketplace is satisfied each time they complete a task in the name of the Lord and according to His command. How you know you have scored a huge point in God concerning your assignment is the divine satisfaction in the form of peace that pleasantly floods your soul upon completing a task.

Of course, this all boils down to constantly ingesting God's word, which is the bread of life by which all men must live (Matthew 4:4).

> **The soul of an apostle of God in the marketplace is satisfied each time they complete a task in the name of the Lord and according to His command.**

THE TABLE OF DEMONS

The table of demons is where vanity, vainglory, wealth, and riches are served in exchange for the soul of man. It is the place where the costliest trading, commerce, and transactions take place. Nebuchadnezzar's table that we have earlier considered is a type of the table of demons because, as we have also already considered, Babylon is a haven for all sorts of fallen, foul, and unclean spirits. This was why Daniel and his comrades refused to dine from it. Let's consider again,

> *And he shouted with a mighty voice, she is fallen! Mighty Babylon is fallen! She has become a resort and dwelling place for demons, a dungeon haunted by every loathsome spirit, an abode for every filthy and detestable bird. For* **ALL NATIONS HAVE DRUNK THE WINE** *of her passionate unchastity, and* **THE RULERS AND LEADERS OF THE EARTH** *have joined with her in committing fornication (idolatry), and the* **BUSINESSMEN OF THE EARTH HAVE BECOME RICH WITH THE WEALTH OF HER EXCESSIVE LUXURY AND WANTONNESS.** (Revelation 18:2-3, AMP, emphasis added)

Note that the personification of Babylon spoken of here is more systemic than it is individualistic. This is a succinct depiction of a demonic system that creates the platform for nations, rulers and leaders of the earth and the business magnates of the earth to exchange their souls for riches and wealth spawned by iniquity. It is a table where worldly buffet is served by legions of demonic waiters, and the cost is the soul of the consumer. How do I know this? Carefully consider the following passage of Scripture:

> *Their merchandise is of gold, silver, precious stones, and pearls; of fine linen, purple, silk, and scarlet [stuffs]; all kinds of scented wood, all sorts of articles of ivory, all varieties of objects of costly woods, bronze, iron, and marble; Of cinnamon, spices, incense, ointment and perfume, and frankincense, of wine and olive oil, fine flour and wheat; of cattle and sheep, horses and conveyances; and of slaves (the bodies) and* SOULS OF MEN! THE RIPE FRUITS AND DELICACIES FOR WHICH YOUR SOUL LONGED *have gone from you, and all your luxuries and dainties, your elegance and splendor are lost to you, never again to be recovered or experienced!* (Revelation 18:12-14, AMP, emphasis added)

WHAT THIS MEANS

This means the work of the apostle in the market of nations has been cut out for them by God; as they have drunk the Lord's Cup and eaten at the Lord's Table - practically offering their souls in covenant and worship to the Lord. The onus is on them to reach out to the nations, rulers, and leaders of the earth and the business magnates of the earth to ensure they break demonic manacles from their souls.

Yes, I am talking about bringing the Lord's deliverance to those who have cut covenants with foul spirits directly or tangentially: people who themselves know they have been so deeply involved with demons that only an act of God's sovereign mercy can save them. These folks number in the countless millions, are spread across all walks of life would seldom make it to the four walls of the church. It is the apostles that have been stationed in the different curves and corners of the marketplace that can be used by God to reach out to them.

Your boss, colleague, business partner, customer, etc., who is not saved is a mission ground. You can take apostolic initiative and prayerfully, consistently reach to them until they drink the Lord's cup and eat at the Lord's Table! Working on a soul in the clutch of demons, especially through a covenant, is like digging a well. You do not stop until you see water! This type of evangelism demands more than sharing tracts and talking to someone about Jesus (as needful as these are). It is engaging the heavens almost obstinately until the captive souls have been won over. This was what Jesus did when He saw the devil, wickedly poised in the shadows and ready swoop on Peter's soul. Jesus prayed intensely before speaking to Peter about it (Luke 22: 31-32).

10

THE GOAL IS SOULS; THE MEANS IS GOLD

To be effective apostles of God in the marketplace, the believer needs to understand the purpose of and how to use the primary tools of money, fame, and power. These are very much needed in the apostolic conquest of the twin platforms of the marketplace of the nations.

MONEY, FAME, AND POWER: THE APOSTOLIC PERSPECTIVE

Let me say without prevarication: there is nothing inherently evil or ungodly about money, fame, and power.

MONEY

Money is simply a legal tender, a measure, and store of value with which goods and services can be smoothly exchanged. It is one of man's greatest inventions. With money, the cumbersome, inefficient barter system by which goods and services were exchanged in ancient times was successfully ended. In the twenty-first century, with the aid of the internet, money has even been further developed to the point where it has become digital.

Meaning, with just the click of a few buttons, money can change hands and facilitate the exchange of goods and services from one part of the world to another – someone in Ogbomosho in Nigeria can successfully buy and pay for a good or service in Hyderabad in India and vice versa. For want of space, we shall not consider the onerous technicalities by which money is created, circulated, and regulated among the nations of the world. However, it is very important to note that what makes money powerful is not its shape, texture, hue or size but that it has been imbued with the exclusive ability to buy – otherwise known as *buying power*. I tell you, as far as the material world goes, the buying power that money has makes it one of the greatest forces under heaven. Something with such an enormous power can be used to pay for anything that is for sale, which is why it has become so many people's obsession – they feel if they can acquire lots of it, they will be able to buy anything they want.

Money is feral – like fire, it can cook and burn; like electric power, it can electrocute and electrify. This means it can both be disastrous and valuable, depending on how it is handled. By design, money is meant to be a tool like a sledgehammer, water heater, toothbrush, and glass cup. But because of the enormous power it possesses, it can, like wild tides, overflow its banks and latch on to the heart of man like a leech or virulent parasite; provoking inordinate love and affection for it and building a throne (control centre) for itself within the heart

> To be effective apostles of God in the marketplace, the believer needs to understand the purpose of and how to use the primary tools of money, fame, and power.

of man. Once the heart of man which has been designed to love only God and fellow humans begins to love money, a malignant aberration called *the root of all evils* is established. The root of all evils will yield the trees of all evil with time. When this happens, a person loses their soul.

This is why the Bible declares in unmistakable terms,

> *'For* **THE LOVE OF MONEY IS A ROOT OF ALL EVILS;** *it is through this craving that some have been led astray and have wandered from the faith and pierced themselves through with many acute [mental] pangs.'* (1 Timothy 6:10, AMP, emphasis added)

The spirit force that catalyses the love for money in the heart of man is called Mammon! Money is not Mammon, and money is not evil.

So,

MONEY IS NOT EQUAL TO THE ROOT OF ALL EVILS

MONEY IS NOT EQUAL TO MAMMON

But,

MONEY + MAMMON + THE HEART OF MAN = THE ROOT OF ALL EVILS

> **Money is feral - like fire, it can cook and burn; like electric power, it can electrocute and electrify**

As earlier stated, money is like fire which is a tool of destruction in the hands of an arsonist and a tool of construction in the hands of a blacksmith.

Jesus said,

> No one can serve two masters, for either he will hate the one and love the other, or he will stand by and be devoted to the one and despise and be against the other. You cannot serve God and mammon (deceitful riches, money, possessions, or whatever you trust in). (Matthew 6:24, AMP)

It is simple: a man who loves money cannot love God. A man who loves God cannot love money. A man who loves God will definitely trust in and serve God. Whereas a man that loves money will inevitably trust in and serve Mammon. A man who trusts in and serves God will sell anything and give up all his possessions to move the cause of His kingdom forward (an example is the early Christians who sold their possessions to execute God's will on earth [Acts 4: 34-25]). A man who loves money will give up God to gain money or material possessions (an example is Judas Iscariot, who sold Jesus for thirty pieces of silver [Matthew 26:15]).

> It is simple: a man who loves money cannot love God. A man who loves God cannot love money

FAME

> Now there was a man in their synagogue with an unclean spirit. And he cried out, saying, "Let us alone! What have we to do with You, Jesus of Nazareth? Did you come to destroy us? I know who you are — the Holy One of God!" But Jesus rebuked him, saying, "Be quiet, and come out of

him!" And when the unclean spirit had convulsed him and cried out with a loud voice, he came out of him. Then they were all amazed, so that they questioned among themselves, saying, "What is this? What new doctrine is this? For with authority He commands even the unclean spirits, and they obey Him." **AND IMMEDIATELY HIS FAME SPREAD THROUGHOUT ALL THE REGION AROUND GALILEE.** (Mark 1:23-28, NKJV, emphasis added)

From the passage above, it is clear that fame does not exist in a vacuum. It is the by-product of a process. Fame is the massive recognition and honour that one gets among many people after they have done something extraordinary or achieved a great feat. So, a famous person is recognised, celebrated, and honoured by many people for doing one or more great things.

> So, fame is not evil. In short, fame was a tool to Jesus because the more His fame spread the more people He reached for God.

From the passage above, Jesus supernaturally cast out an evil spirit from a man in the presence of people who were utterly wowed. Now, this was a remarkable feat, an impossible achievement, so to speak. This immediately brought him recognition among both those present and those who heard about it. It made Him famous! You see, there was not a single miracle that Jesus performed on impulse. Everything He ever did, including the feat in the passage above was as a result of God's direct command (John 5:19)! It is therefore, safe to say that fame is a direct consequence of executing God's will. So, fame is not evil. In short, fame was a tool to Jesus because the more His fame spread the more people He reached for God.

Watchman Nee once said, and I paraphrase, "There is a degree of vanity attached to any kind of success whether physical or spiritual." Whether a person's business is experiencing tremendous growth or a ministry is exploding with a great harvest of souls into the kingdom, there is a shadow of vanity that goes with the fame it attracts. It behoves the servant of God, therefore, to guard their heart with all diligence so that the vanity that accompanies fame does not compromise the intensity of love they have for God which propels them to give their best to execute His will.

> Fame is purely external because it is people's reaction to something God uses His servant to do. The best way to deal with fame, therefore, is to make sure it remains external.

Fame is purely external because it is people's reaction to something God uses His servant to do. The best way to deal with fame, therefore, is to make sure it remains external. It should never be allowed to get into a person's heart because if it does, it becomes poison. It's like bathing soap that is strictly meant to be used on the skin; the same becomes poison when ingested deliberately or indeliberately.

POWER

Power is simply the ability to do. The power of God is the ability God releases to a person to transform in character to become like Him and execute His will on earth. The power of God enables God's servant to carry out their God-given tasks. The power of God works within the believer's heart to transform them and on their hands to carry out and fulfil God's instructions. The power of God, depending on the nature of the assignment, enables God's servants to overcome character flaws and preach the gospel, open people up to salvation, heal the sick, raise the dead, get wealth, cast out devils, overcome obstacles, etc. In short, it is impossible to lead the Christian life without the power of God, much less talk of doing His will. Only one person dispenses God's power: His name is the Holy Spirit (Acts 1.8).

The British historian and moralist Lord John Acton said, "Power tends to corrupt, and absolute power tends to corrupt absolutely." Well, not the power of God! The power of God brings the best out of whomever or whatever it comes in contact with. Whatever is done without God's power can only be bland, natural, and impotent at best! Yet, the successes that come as a result of putting God's power to use can poison one's heart.

THE APOSTOLIC PERSPECTIVE

As God's apostles – messengers – we must always defer to the leadership of the Holy Spirit to help us bear in mind that we are stewards and that nothing is really ours, though we have full access to the excesses of His bounty. And that in our journey of faith and daily execution of His will, money, fame, and power and the successes they bring should only pass through our hands and not touch our hearts. One thing is clear from the short notes on money, fame, and power above: the best way to handle all three is to consistently and diligently guard one's heart in the place of prayer. Money, fame, and power are for propagating the gospel and not for the destruction of our souls.

It is practically impossible to move God's kingdom on earth without power and money. For those whose God-given assignments require them to remain conspicuous in the public eye, it is impossible to execute God's will without having to deal with fame. So if we set our affections on the things above always, make pleasing God our number one priority, and guard our hearts diligently, we will be free from the snares and attachments connected to the successes that money, fame, and power bring!

May we continue to use the tools in this world to execute God's will and not get engrossed in them. Remember, nothing else should fill your heart apart from the love of God, which in turn should inspire you to love your fellow man unconditionally. Love precedes service. Service carried out on the foundation of God's love never goes wrong. The heart that is not filled with God's love will be filled with the love of money and, by extension, the love of the world. The love of money inspires unconditional service to Mammon - in which the souls of people are manipulated for personal gain. As essential as this is, many churches and

> **Money, fame, and power are for propagating the gospel and not for the destruction of our souls.**

ministries in our day with intercontinental reach are powered by Mammon. The name of Jesus is thrown around and slapped on everything these churches and ministries do, but the Spirit of Christ is absent from the architecture of these Christian centres. Hence, what these centres churn out is nothing but a high voltage of ungodliness. These centres sadly litter our landscape. They can only be put out of business if we insist on yielding to the government of God and influencing others to do the same one soul at a time.

Again, it is our duty, not God's, to keep anything that can poison our hearts from gaining access therein. This is the core of the apostolic culture, which is the infrastructure upon which any impactful apostolic work can be built. Money, fame, and power should be used as resources to enhance our strategic apostleship, in getting His kingdom to come and His will aggressively done on earth as it is in heaven, and not for personal aggrandizement and decoration, which will end in deterioration. A sure way to win by righteousness is to use money, fame, and power as tools. A sure way to lose by ungodliness is to abuse them!

I have addressed strategic apostleship and kingdom service in my book GO INTO ALL THE WORLD.

TRUE RICHES OF THE KINGDOM

> *He who is faithful in a very little [thing] is faithful also in much, and he who is dishonest and unjust in a very little [thing] is dishonest and unjust also in much. Therefore if you have*

> not been faithful in the [case of] unrighteous mammon (deceitful riches, money, possessions), who will entrust to you the true riches? (Luke 16:10-11, AMP)

Concerning the believer's measure in Christ, I must quickly add that it is not a static reality. It is scalable (progressive or retrogressive) depending on the believer's faithfulness. God might ordain a believer to take on a great task, but He does not drop everything in their lap. He gradually and systematically commits little things into their hands to test their level of faithfulness until they are faithful enough to handle much.

> True riches are only available in Christ, and they cause a believer to overflow with the very abundance of God.

Before Joseph became second in command to Pharaoh, he faithfully managed his father's little business and Potiphar's household.

For the apostles in the marketplace, one of the things they would have to master is unrighteous mammon which the passage above describes as deceitful riches, money, and possessions. I have briefly touched on mammon already. I would like to expand a little more on it here. But first, the Bible in the passage above clearly establishes that material riches, money, and possessions (which make up the pulse of today's socio-economic world) are not true riches. So, we shall concurrently look more into what mammon is and what true riches are.

The phrase *true riches* is *huperperisseuo* in Greek, and it means to cause someone to overflow with something, to be present in increasingly greater measures. So true riches are only available in Christ, and they cause a believer to overflow with the very abundance of God. We earlier considered how Joseph was a prosperous man not because he had physical possessions but because the Lord was with him. True riches are gold mined from God and not gold mined from the dust of the ground. Those who are only rich in gold mined from the dust of the ground are actually poor. Jesus Christ fiercely declared,

> *Because you say, 'I AM RICH, HAVE BECOME WEALTHY, AND HAVE NEED OF NOTHING' — AND DO NOT KNOW THAT YOU ARE WRETCHED, MISERABLE, POOR, blind, and naked — I COUNSEL YOU TO BUY FROM ME GOLD REFINED IN THE FIRE, THAT YOU MAY BE RICH; and white garments, that you may be clothed, that the shame of your nakedness may not be revealed; and anoint your eyes with eye salve, that you may see* (Revelation 3:17-18, NKJV, emphasis added)

> **Mammon in Greek is *mamonas* and it means wealth personified or avarice (greed) deified. He can only give wealth to those who worship him by the principle of avarice**

Mammon in Greek is *mamonas* and it means wealth personified or avarice (greed) deified. He can only give wealth to those who worship him by the principle of avarice. So, this is essentially the spirit that powers materialism and projects and amplifies gold above God.

Jesus is truth personified and truth deified. He alone can give riches that can preserve man wholly - spirit, soul, and body. Any man who worships Him through the principle of sanctification gets to enjoy His eternal largesse (1 Thessalonians 5:23).

True riches are riches based on, spawned, and produced by truth. Jesus is truth. The true riches of the kingdom are not found on the surface - a shallow relationship with God as defined by materialism. They are found in the very depths of God. In God is Christ, who is an inexhaustible gold mine of eternally incorruptible riches. The Holy Spirit is the only Miner capable of mining the depths of God to bring out His riches for the believer's eternal profiting and benefit. True riches are God's grace, knowledge, understanding, wisdom, authority, and power - all of which are embodied and personified by Christ (Romans 2:4, 9:23, 11:12, 11:33; Ephesians 1:7,18, 2:7, 3:8, 16; Philippians 4:19, Colossians 1:27, 2:2).

> Jesus is truth personified and truth deified. He alone can give riches that can preserve man wholly - spirit, soul, and body.

So, true riches are essentially the substance of the life, nature, and character of God mined by the Spirit of truth (John 14:17) and transmitted into the believer's reins in order to stuff them with more and more of God until they fully become like Him. The Holy Spirit (Spirit of truth) is the miner of the deep riches of God (1 Corinthians 2:10). The Holy Spirit counteracts mammon and delivers the riches of God through knowledge (1 Corinthians 2:12).

Even reproach, contempt, abuse, and shame that come to the believer on account of their faith in Jesus Christ are part of the true riches (Hebrews 11:26).

> True riches are riches based on, spawned, and produced by truth. Jesus is truth.

GOLD FROM THE DUST, GOLD FROM GOD, AND THE SOULS OF MEN

The apostolic ministry in the marketplace is operated with gold from the dust, gold from God interlocked for profiting through winning the souls of men.

The gold from the dust which is primarily managed by mammon creates the material resource base for apostolic conquest of the marketplace.

Yes, money, material riches, and possessions are much needed in penetrating every walk of life and people system with the message of the kingdom of Lord Jesus Christ. As such, apostles in the marketplace need to be directly involved with the processes of production and value creation; and to be savvy with cutting edge skills and knowledge that can be used to create material wealth. This would, in turn, be used to finance and propagate the gospel of the kingdom within the marketplace. I am talking about Christian entrepreneurs, infopreneurs, technopreneurs, employees, traders, artisans, employees, and leaders of thought, managers in private and public sectors, etc., rising in obedience and preaching Christ crucified within their spheres of influence.

> Apostles in the marketplace need to be directly involved with the processes of production and value creation; and to be savvy with cutting edge skills and knowledge that can be used to create material wealth.

Much more, we need true riches to be able to use unrighteous mammon as a tool. Those who do not have true riches are those who worship and serve mammon because the lordship of Christ is not in force in their lives.

Not everyone in Christ would be a millionaire and billionaire because the material and spiritual resources we get are directly proportional to our measures in Christ. But everyone would get enough to fulfil their God-given assignment, especially for those whose primary operation is on the governmental platform of the marketplace. They would need to be more strategically positioned in the place of authority to push God's agenda in their sphere of influence than they would need material riches.

The proper use of unrighteous mammon creates platforms that make direct contact with unbelievers possible, but it is true riches that facilitate the deliverance of the souls of unbelievers from the kingdom of darkness into the kingdom of God. Therefore, though material riches are important, true riches are more important for the believer to have and wield.

I speak as one who has been shown mercy by the Lord to know through experience that material resources are important in propagating the gospel, but true riches are more important when it comes to engaging souls in the name of the Lord. This is why it is good to set up humanitarian systems like NGOs and foundations etc., to feed the hungry, and reach out to the poor and sick with material aids. But after all these, Christ crucified must be preached to these folks in word and deed. It is easier to preach Christ to a hungry man after giving him food. It is easier to preach Christ to an affluent man who is under demonic oppression after sending the demons packing in the name of the Lord Jesus. It is easier to preach Christ to a business partner who sees that for some strange reason you have chosen not to cut corners and allow greed take the place of God in your dealings but have remained righteous in all your dealings with them. It is easier to preach to someone from whom you have refused to take a bribe after they have attempted to bribe you eleven times.

> Material resources are important in propagating the gospel, but true riches are more important when it comes to engaging souls in the name of the Lord.

11

RIGHTEOUS STEWARDSHIP

As each one has received a GIFT, MINISTER it to one another, as good STEWARDS of the manifold GRACE of God. (1 Peter 4:1, NKJV, emphasis added)

Note the words *gift, minister, stewards,* and *grace* are vital in carrying out our God-given assignment in the marketplace of nations. This is because everyone in Christ has got a gift from God with which they have to minister (serve) Him through serving people as stewards of the grace of God.

The concept of stewardship is hundred percent access with zero percent ownership. A good steward of the grace of God knows they do not personally own anything but have access to all of God's riches and act accordingly. A bad steward of God's grace knows they do not personally own anything but have access to all of God's riches yet do not act accordingly.

The purpose of a gift (resources, power, influence, etc.), according to the verse of Scripture above, is to minister it to one another. This means a gift is not primarily meant for the receiver but for others. As we prioritise the service of God through serving others, we practically become selfless, and that is the whole point of being good stewards of the grace of God. The design of the service protocol, as it has to do with dispensing the grace of God to others, is meant to be all about God and nothing about us. The moment we begin to use God's gift for personal aggrandizement is when we breach the protocol of kingdom service.

> The concept of stewardship is hundred percent access with zero percent ownership. A good steward of the grace of God knows they do not personally own anything but have access to all of God's riches and act accordingly.

The chief executive officer of a publicly operated bank is a steward. He has access to all the bank's capital but does not own it. The bank is owned by the shareholders. The CEO can therefore vote capital at their discretion to bring more profit to the shareholders while their personal needs are met by the remuneration packages agreed upon by the shareholders. It is a high crime for the CEO to use the bank's capital for their personal gain. Such a crime attracts harsh punishments that could end up in lengthy prison time. This is a rough human example.

If the CEO of a bank set up by human beings is this regulated, how much more the steward of the grace of God? This is where many believers miss it. They mistake the things that are entrusted to them by God as their personal belongings. We studied about Cain earlier in this book, and we saw how that when he strayed from God's presence, he established a civilisation independent of God in which men began to own things. Personal ownership is a symptom of a lack of submission to God.

A believer who accepts the lordship of Jesus Christ knows that the Lord possesses not just heaven and earth but their very soul. Abraham, the patriarch of faith, gave a tithe to King Melchizedek based on the revelation he received of God's lordship. It is worthy of note that in the sequence of events that led to Abraham giving a tithe to King Melchizedek, King Melchizedek blessed Abraham before (Genesis 14:18) Abraham gave him tithe (Genesis 14:20) and not after. Why is this important? Because King Melchizedek's blessing of Abraham was not an atmospheric reaction to Abraham's giving. It was a preemptive, unconditional gesture of goodwill (very consistent with the operation of God in the New Covenant). Abraham's tithe did not inspire the blessing. The blessing inspired Abraham's tithe.

Therefore, what was the blessing that King Melchizedek pronounced on Abraham? It was thus:

> *"Blessed be Abram of God Most High,*
> *POSSESSOR OF HEAVEN AND EARTH;*
> *And blessed be God Most High,*
> *Who has delivered your enemies into your hand."*
> (Genesis 14:19-20, NKJV, emphasis added)

Note the phrases: *God Most High and possessor of heaven and earth.*

RIGHTEOUS STEWARDSHIP

God Most High means the greatest and the most exalted God. Possessor of heaven and earth means God owned and still owns heaven and everything in it and the world and everything in it. This also means He lacks nothing and needs nothing. Possessor means owner. And owner is what the word LORD means. King Melchizedek simply revealed the Lordship of God to Abraham. By the sheer force of this revelation, Abraham gave a tithe of all that he had at that moment. Abraham's tithe was not merely him parting ways with ten per-cent of his possessions out of obligation or emotion. It was him deeply and sturdily acknowledging the lordship, ownership, and if you will, possessorship of God who owned everything in heaven and earth, including him. The role of the priest in the Old Testament was to act as an intermediary between man and God. Consequently, Abraham giving ten per cent to King Melchizedek was him giving to God, knowing fully well that God owned him and the 90% left.

> A believer who accepts the lordship of Jesus Christ knows that the Lord possesses not just heaven and earth but their very soul.

How do I know that Abraham submitted to God's lordship as presented by King Melchizedek?

Simple.

Shortly after meeting King Melchizedek, Abraham met with the king of Sodom, who made a rather strange proposal to him to which Abraham replied thus:

Now the king of Sodom said to Abram, "Give me the persons, and take the goods for yourself." But Abram said to the king of

Sodom, "I HAVE RAISED MY HAND TO THE LORD, GOD MOST HIGH, THE POSSESSOR OF HEAVEN AND EARTH, that I will take nothing, from a thread to a sandal strap, and that I will not take anything that is yours, lest you should say, 'I have made Abram rich' — except only what the young men have eaten, and the portion of the men who went with me: Aner, Eshcol, and Mamre; let them take their portion." (Genesis 14:21-24, NKJV)

From the passage above, you can see Abraham quoting King Melchizedek verbatim. Abraham took it to the next level by saying *I HAVE RAISED MY HAND TO THE LORD...* The phrase *I have raised my hand,* is what the Hebrew word *YADAH* means, from which Judah is taken. Yadah means to lift one's hand in surrender, which is loosely translated as praise or worship. This is because to praise and worship God effectively with our being and substance, a revelation of His *most highness* and lordship must be caught. So, the phrase *I HAVE RAISED MY HAND TO THE LORD* means I have acknowledged the lordship of God. And if you have recognised and submitted to the lordship of God, it means He does not only own you and ten per cent of your possession, but owns you and a hundred per cent of your possession. It was with this understanding that Abraham gave.

Tithe means ten per cent, but its essence is deeper than that. This is because Abraham did not give tithe in obedience to a command from God; he gave because he caught a profound revelation of God's lordship stretching from heaven to earth, to him and all he had. He understood that God owned heaven one hundred per cent, earth one hundred per cent, him and everything he had one hundred per cent.

A steward is not an owner but a manager. A steward does not personally own anything but has access to everything. It is like being the president of a country. The president of America is a steward of America's wealth and power. He has access to all of America's wealth and power but does not personally own them. He does not need to worry about his personal needs because they are being taken care of by the commonwealth of his nation. The president of America can give money and other favours to other countries on behalf of his country within the ambit of the laws guiding the extent of the exercise of the powers of his office. If the American president uses his nation's commonwealth for personal aggrandizement, he is liable to be punished because he has abused his power.

GIVING AND THE LORDSHIP OF JESUS CHRIST

As stewards of God, we have access to all of God's riches even though He owns everything, including us. This means every resource that comes to our hands is not primarily ours to claim. It is the Lord's. This revelation can only be caught in deep and consistent communion with God. The revelation of the lordship of Jesus Christ is not received in one contact. It is received and ingested on an incremental basis. When the Lord Jesus intercepted Saul (Paul) on his way to Damascus, the Lord commissioned him into kingdom service saying,

> *But rise and stand on your feet; for I have appeared to you for this purpose, to make you a minister and* **A WITNESS BOTH OF THE**

THINGS WHICH YOU HAVE SEEN AND OF THE THINGS WHICH I WILL YET REVEAL TO YOU. (Acts 26:16, NKJV, emphasis mine)

Note that the Lord did not reveal everything to Saul at once because he did not have the capacity to bear it all at the time.

God gradually teaches us about His lordship and empowers us by His Spirit to respond accordingly. Oh, yes, no one can catch a revelation of the lordship of Jesus Christ except it is given to them by the Holy Spirit. The Bible says

> Giving is proof of love. You can't love someone without giving to them. God Himself loved us, and that was why He gave His only begotten Son.

...*no one can say that Jesus is Lord except by the Holy Spirit* (1 Corinthians 12:3, NKJV)

Indeed, no one can acknowledge the lordship of Jesus Christ except by the enablement of the Holy Spirit!

Anyone who therefore acknowledges the lordship of Jesus Christ knows that they do not own anything as everything they own belongs to Him. When they give to His cause, they do not do so out of obligation but in submission to His lordship. This brings great pleasure to Him, and this is what worship is: any action or inaction that brings pleasure to God.

Giving is proof of love. You can't love someone without giving to them. God Himself loved us, and that was why He gave His only begotten son (John 3:16). So, you can't say you love God and not give back to Him (His cause.) Like Abraham gave after he was blessed by Melchizedek, we do not give to be blessed, but we are blessed, so we give.

The law in the Old Testament has been replaced by the government of God in the New Testament, the administrator of which is the Holy Spirit. In the New Testament, the Holy Spirit teaches us how to obey God every step of the way as we execute His will on earth.

THE GOAL OF STEWARDSHIP IS TO GIVE HUNDRED PERCENT TO GOD ALWAYS!

The journey of Abraham's giving did not stop at ten percent. It progressed to a hundred percent! When he gave ten percent that was the beginning of the journey. It was not the best he could do, but it was a step in the right direction. He grew in his walk with God that God demanded a hundred percent - Isaac, the son of promise whom he waited twenty-five years to have and upon whom the future of his lineage depended. But because he had grown well in walking with God and acknowledging His lordship, he knew even Isaac belonged to God. It was very hard, no doubt. This was a hundred percent! This means ten percent is really elementary!

Giving should be love-motivated, not dividend-inspired. You do not give to receive anything from God. You should give because you love Him and accept His lordship over your life. Giving to God is not merely an investment decision in which you expect a handsome return. No, it is all about love for God and unreserved acceptance of His lordship.

> Giving should be love-motivated, not dividend-inspired. You do not give to receive anything from God. You should give because you love Him and accept His lordship over your life.

WHAT IS A HUNDRED PERCENT?

We achieve hundred per cent giving when we have grown in our acknowledgement and submission to the lordship of Christ. When the Lord can demand anything from us. This is when we fully become good stewards of God's grace. At this point, we stop seeing anything as ours but His. That you give does not make you a steward. If you still lay claim to things or resources given to you by God as yours, you are yet to step into stewardship. Stewardship is the highest level of kingdom resource management. Giving ten per cent does not make us stewards. Giving our 'Isaac' does! God dared ask Abraham for Isaac because He knew Abraham had the capacity to give up Isaac.

THE EARLY CHURCH CONQUERED THE WORLD BECAUSE THEY GAVE HUNDRED PERCENT, SO SHOULD WE!

The early church did not have mammoth buildings, huge financial resources, a standing army, media power, and the likes. Yet, in a few centuries, they conquered every inch of the then known world. How did they do it?

Now let's consider this together:

RIGHTEOUS STEWARDSHIP

> *Now the multitude of those who believed were of one heart and one soul;* NEITHER DID ANYONE SAY THAT ANY OF THE THINGS HE POSSESSED WAS HIS OWN, *but they had all things in common. And with great power the apostles gave witness to the resurrection of the Lord Jesus. And great grace was upon them all. Nor was there anyone among them who lacked;* FOR ALL WHO WERE POSSESSORS OF LANDS OR HOUSES SOLD THEM, AND BROUGHT THE PROCEEDS OF THE THINGS THAT WERE SOLD, AND LAID THEM AT THE APOSTLES' FEET; AND THEY DISTRIBUTED TO EACH AS ANYONE HAD NEED. (Acts 4:32-35, NKJV, emphasis added)

I hope the highlighted portions of the passage above are clear enough. One word comes to mind after reading this: STEWARDSHIP! The church was young at the time, but their understanding of Christ's lordship was very mature. They gave hundred per cent.

The church historian and theologian, David Pawson, said concerning the conquest of the world by the early church (paraphrased):

> *They won a physical battle over suffering, won a mental battle over heresy, and a spiritual battle over other religions. They won that battle because they outlived, outthought, and outdied everyone else. Beginning with a*

handful of fishermen, Christianity spread throughout the then known world until it replaced every other religion. They did it without an army, but they fought well. They did it without money, they did it without influential people, and did it with all the might and power of a Roman Empire against them. They brought Christianity from the capital of the sacred world (Jerusalem) to Rome (the capital of the secular world). They had been greatly helped by the Roman roads, straight roads leading right around the Mediterranean world. They were greatly helped by the fact that everyone spoke one common language (the Greek language). They were greatly helped by the fact that there was peace (the famous Pax Romana [Latin for "Roman Peace"] is a roughly 200-year-long period in Roman history which is identified with increased and sustained inner hegemonic peace and stability) that ensured they could travel from country to country without passports, visas, or all the modern paraphernalia of travel that missionaries have to battle with.

Yes, the early believers were helped by the fact that the whole empire was morally and spiritually sick. Nevertheless, it is still an astonishing triumph. The church was spread by missionaries (apostles), ordinary men and women, commercial travellers who took the gospel everywhere they went. The early church did not have influential people in society, they had no denominational buildings, they had no headquarters, they had no financial resources. They had just simple groups they called churches, with each having elders to

> serve them spiritually and deacons to serve them practically. The apostles moved between the churches, planted new congregations, and acted as pioneers and evangelists who preached the gospel. They grew till the pagan temples were deserted; the Roman Empire was conquered with the Roman emperor himself in church – worshipping Jesus Christ!

The early church folks were a highly strategic army of stewards of the grace of God who heavily relied on the wisdom and power of God to spread the gospel to every corner of their world. We are even more advantaged than they were because over two thousand years later, we have material and financial resources that can be used to subdue the marketplace of the nations!

IT IS REQUIRED FOR STEWARDS TO BE FAITHFUL

> *Moreover, it is required in stewards that one be found faithful* (1 Corinthians 4:2, NKJV)

The word faithful is *pistis* in Greek, and it means trustworthiness! We begin our journey of faith by trusting in God. We then build a solid relationship with God long enough for Him to install His character infrastructure within us until we become worthy of His trust. This is when we will have grown well enough in our journey of faith to engage higher resources in His name. He tests us with little opportunities, resources, and gifts. If we manage them well, He increases the consignments until He can entrust us with His very heartbeat – the destiny of nations spread across all walks of life. So, we start by trusting God, and we gain His trust by becoming trustworthy through seasons of tests that He entirely determines. Then, He can entrust us with great and mighty things.

It is true that God is not limited by time, but we are. Time is a game-changer on this side of eternity. It takes time to build a consistent history of trustworthiness with God. In my experience, it takes about a decade (this is not a doctrine, just experience) of incessant trials and travails for a conviction to fructify. It takes years for God to fully possess the vessel of His apostle before He sends them forth to represent Him and fills their hands with His great resources. It costs God nothing to promote a man *overnight* since He can open doors that no man can shut and shut doors that no man can open. But since His promotion system does not support profligacy, He would rather take His time to work on the vessel to show forth His glory among the nations.

> We begin our journey of faith by trusting in God. We then build a solid relationship with God long enough for Him to install His character infrastructure within us until we become worthy of His trust.

We laboured for at least twelve years before the Lord finally opened the door for international ministry to the body of Christ for us. Prior to this time, He practically placed an embargo on our going outside the shores of our home country Nigeria for the purpose of ministering to His body. He practically made us turn down countless invitations. But in His own time, He made everything beautiful. Looking back now, I am forever grateful that the Lord locked us down to take root downward so we can bear fruit upward. Thank the Lord Jesus for staying with us until we became trustworthy to become stewards of His grace.

The riches of the Lord cannot be searched out. He is that wealthy! Yet He is flawlessly efficient – He is not in a hurry to entrust a man with His riches until the man is proven to be trustworthy. The Lord is particular about faithfulness in the stewardship of His grace because the slightest abuse of it could mangle a generation and destroy the souls of those involved. There are few men He can entrust with the hallowed task of purposefully sharing the burden of His wealth for the liberations of nations in the marketplace. The criterion is faithfulness!

> The riches of the Lord cannot be searched out. He is that wealthy! Yet He is flawlessly efficient - He is not in a hurry to entrust a man with His riches until the man is proven to be trustworthy.

Dear Christian soldier and apostle of the Lord Jesus Christ in the marketplace, do not abandon the little the Lord has commissioned you to do. The Lord is an expert in multiplying the little that has been faithfully executed in His name into something that towers to the high heavens. Much more than trusting in the Lord, the Lord is seeking for those He too can trust!

12

YOU ARE NOT OUTNUMBERED: THE MAJORITY OF ONE WITH GOD!

Now the king of Syria was making war against Israel; and he consulted with his servants, saying, "My camp will be in such and such a place." And the man of God sent to the king of Israel, saying, "Beware that you do not pass this place, for the Syrians are coming down there." Then the king of Israel sent someone to the place of which the man of God had told him. Thus he warned him, and he was watchful there, not just once or twice. Therefore the heart of the king of Syria was greatly troubled by this thing; and he called his servants and said to them, "Will you not show me which of us is for the king of Israel?"

And one of his servants said, "None, my lord, O king; but Elisha, the prophet who is in Israel, tells the king of Israel the words that you speak in your bedroom."

> *So he said, "Go and see where he is, that I may send and get him."*
>
> *And it was told him, saying, "Surely he is in Dothan."*
>
> *Therefore he sent horses and chariots and a great army there, and they came by night and surrounded the city. And when the servant of the man of God arose early and went out, there was an army, surrounding the city with horses and chariots. And his servant said to him, "Alas, my master! What shall we do?" So he answered, "Do not fear, for those who are with us are more than those who are with them." And Elisha prayed, and said, "Lord, I pray, open his eyes that he may see." Then the Lord opened the eyes of the young man, and he saw. And behold, the mountain was full of horses and chariots of fire all around Elisha. So when the Syrians came down to him, Elisha prayed to the Lord, and said, "Strike this people, I pray, with blindness." And He struck them with blindness according to the word of Elisha.* (2 Kings 6:8-18, NKJV)

This beautiful passage captures the war games that the king of Syria tried to play against Israel that blew up in his face. Time and again, the king of Syria would draw up sophisticated attack plans against Israel, but somehow, the full details of his offensive plan would fall on the ears of the king of Israel. One time, two times, three times, and his curiosity was piqued. He was forced to think there were saboteurs within his command. Upon thorough investigation, he found out that the person responsible for the full broadcast of his offensive plans against Israel to the king of Israel was someone who had never been to the premises of his palace before but was privy to every whisper he made in his bedroom. The name of the varmint who caused all of Syria's problems was the man of God, Elisha. With his prophetic insight into every move of Syria's king, Syria did not stand a chance against Israel.

The king of Syria quickly swung into action to silence Elisha forever. He sent spies to locate Elisha's abode and wasted no time in sending a ferocious killer squad to surround him, pound him, and round him up. They marched all night in order to successfully apprehend the man of God. This was a frantic attempt by the king of Syria to leave Israel prophetically defenceless so he can equally surround, pound, and round them up. Alas, he was greatly mistaken.

Elisha's servant awoke in the morning and stepped out to begin his day. He saw an army arrayed against his master. He went back in to report to his master because, in his thinking, he and his master were obviously outmanned and outnumbered. But he too was greatly mistaken as the man of God prayed to God to open his eyes to see the superior army poised on chariots of fire straight from heaven, who surrounded the Syrian troops. The Syrian chariots and horses were outnumbered by the fiery chariots and horses of God. So, the *surrounders* became the surrounded. Elisha and his servant were in the company of Lord of hosts, and that was all that mattered. Elisha's being with God made the whole Syrian horde the minority, and he the majority. The Syrian troops were comprehensively defeated by Elisha's being a man with God who did not hesitate in marshalling heaven's resources to dwarf the Syrians! Hence my assertion: one with God is the majority! When Elisha's servant's eyes were opened to see the heavenly backup against the Syrians, his wobbly confidence in the God of his master was transmuted to mount Zion that cannot be moved. And at showdown, the Syrian troops had no option than to bend the knee.

WHO CAN OUTNUMBER GOD?

The answer is no one, from eternity to eternity!

Why?

Because He is the *Lord of hosts*! We cannot go Scripture after Scripture to consider this popular yet often insufficiently understood title of God for want of space. This title is almost ubiquitous in the Old Testament as it stretches from 1 Samuel to Malachi. Often, we just gloss over it in our Bible study.

> Do you know what it means to be on the side of He who possesses heaven and earth and innumerable hosts? It means being plugged into a power source and authority base that cannot be matched by any force in existence!

What then does it mean for God to be the Lord of hosts? It means God is the owner of innumerable commands, companies, and systems through which He exercises His infinite capabilities, capacities, power, wisdom, and authority. The point of God being the Lord of hosts is not just that He owns and commands innumerable forces; it is that He wields resources with capacities and capabilities that are unmatched from eternity to eternity. And those who partner with Him get to enjoy the services of His hosts. These hosts have incalculable abilities – they can engage flesh and blood, supernatural forces, the elements, and even systems figured within the four corners of the earth. In Elisha's case, the heavenly hosts struck the Syrian troops with blindness; because he was with God!

Do you know what it means to be on the side of He who possesses heaven and earth and innumerable hosts? It means being plugged into a power source and authority base that cannot be matched by any force in existence! God's Prophet Samuel hitched his wagon to God and became a God-backed potentate that successfully warded off attacks on his nation by its enemies. Yes, Israel's foremost enemies, the Philistines were so immobilised and frozen to perennial imbecility throughout the days of Samuel that they did not launch a single attack against Israel while Samuel was its judge. Samuel teamed up with God and made minorities out of formidable foes like the Philistines. The Bible says,

> Whenever we lift our hands in surrender to God, we interlock our faith with His massive capabilities and abilities in a manner that so unstoppably brings His invincibility to bear in our sphere of influence and primary place of assignment.

So the Philistines were subdued, and they did not come anymore into the territory of Israel. And the hand of the Lord was against the Philistines all the days of Samuel. (1 Samuel 7:13, NKJV)

Whenever we lift our hands in surrender to God, we interlock our faith with His massive capabilities and abilities in a manner that so unstoppably brings His invincibility to bear in our sphere of influence and primary place of assignment. We become a majority force against any system we take on in His name.

THE POSSIBILITIES IN OUR DAY

The Lord of hosts worked with men in the Old Testament to bring about the fulfilment of His agenda. He did not usually indwell them because Jesus had not yet died to make this normative. Now that Jesus has died and has made it possible for God to be tabernacled in man, it means man can become the container of matchless abilities and capabilities that God Himself releases into his vessel. This means as long as God resides in a person, that person can bring down any installation of darkness no matter how much of a juggernaut it is.

No matter how impregnable a system looks, God will always empower His human host to breach it. Because the power available to the believer on account of God residing in them is such that it transcends any contradiction and resistance that the devil can ever invent. Consequently, the Bible says,

> **Little children, you are of God [you belong to Him] and have [already] defeated and overcome them [the agents of the antichrist], because He**

> *Who lives in you is greater (mightier) than he who is in the world.* (1 John 4:4, AMP)

This means a man who carries God on his inside is bigger and mightier than all the forces of the world combined. This is not motivational talk. It is practicable truth! It cost God so much to bring forth the new creation. He had to resurrect His Son in order to make it possible for humankind to have eternal life. He expended so much power in resurrecting Jesus from the dead. The Bible says,

> *And [so that you can know and understand] what is the immeasurable and unlimited and surpassing greatness of His power in and for us who believe, as demonstrated in the working of His mighty strength, Which He exerted in Christ when He raised Him from the dead and seated Him at His [own] right hand in the heavenly [places]* (Ephesians 1:19-20, AMP).

This Scripture paints the picture of God investing Himself to raise Jesus from the dead. It is not on record in Scripture that God exerted Himself this much in creating heaven and earth. This is because creation is the work of His hands – and did not

> No matter how impregnable a system looks, God will always empower His human host to breach it. Because the power available to the believer on account of God residing in them is such that it transcends any contradiction and resistance that the devil can ever invent

require the immeasurable and unlimited surpassing greatness of His power to be fabricated. Jesus (who Himself is uncreated God) is not the work of God's hands. So resurrecting Jesus required God to exert Himself prodigiously. This is why the new creation is superior to the old creation – the energy levels by which the two were forged are not the same. The most beautiful part of this process is the fact that God did not only expend the immeasurable and unlimited surpassing greatness of His power to resurrect Jesus alone, He has also made the same power available to those who believe! Wow! Are you a believer? Then this is for you! This power is accessible through faith, consistent prayer (as a lifestyle), and righteousness. The Bible says,

> ...*The earnest (heartfelt, continued)* **PRAYER** *of a* **RIGHTEOUS** *man makes tremendous power available [dynamic in its working].*
> (James 5:16, AMP, emphasis added)

The phrase *the immeasurable and unlimited surpassing greatness* as it has to do with God's power in Greek is *huperballon megethos* and, it roughly translates to *beyond the magnitude of the usual mark, limit*. This means, if there is a glass ceiling, God's power shatters it. If there is demonic limitation, God's power destroys it; if there is a generational curse or hereditary ill will, God's power destroys it. If no one dares rise above certain heights and live, God's power ensures they have more life after surpassing such heights. If no 'Christian' has ever made it in such a line of work or business without compromise, God's power makes it possible to win by righteousness. If no one can have peace without first appeasing the ruler-deity in a territory, God's power reduces the deity to an imbecile. By this power: when a deadly viper bit Paul, he was unhurt; the foundations of the prison were shaken till they vomited the elect of the Lord; kings were slain for blasphemy, sorcerers were made blind and mad for trying to stop the gospel, and the most ruthless resistance against the spread of the gospel of the kingdom of the Lord Jesus Christ was reduced to ashes.

I have seen dark forces fall in my life and ministry. In the marketplace where I am also privileged by God to serve, I have seen seemingly impossible doors open and those bound in covenant with demons discomfited – I have seen gatekeepers and captains of industry bow to the Lord. Plots to harm me and my household have been foiled, and inexplicable systemic and territorial breakthroughs have occurred.

No matter how tough a terrain is, with God, nothing is impossible. The only thing required from God's servant is to fix their gaze on who God is and not what the enemy is doing.

About nineteen years ago when I went for my mandatory national youth service in the ancient city of Kano, Nigeria. I lived with an uncle of mine who was a police officer. My uncle lived in a security community called Bompai Police Barracks, Kano – Nigeria.

As my custom was, I would usually locate a place I could pray alone whenever I went to a new city. So, I went out to a nearby bush to pray. A few weeks after I started praying, I met some teenagers who also made the bush their prayer rendezvous. I was intrigued that teenagers in a police barrack could be as hungry for God as to go to the bush to pray. I enquired from them how they came about their hunger for God, and they told me they were part of a youth fellowship called Hossana Good News Fellowship. My interest was immediately stoked, so I decided to accompany them to the fellowship. I was amazed by what I saw – young men and women, boys and girls, filled with the Spirit and burning in righteousness for God. It was such an incredible sight as my heart rejoiced abundantly in the Lord.

> By this power: when a deadly viper bit Paul, nothing happened to him; the foundations of the prison were shaken till they vomited the elect of the Lord; kings wore slain for blasphemy sorcerers were made blind and mad for trying to stop the gospel, and the most ruthless resistance against the spread of the gospel of the kingdom of the Lord Jesus Christ was reduced to ashes.

The founder of Hossana Good News Fellowship was himself a policeman, named Inspector Garba Usman (of blessed memory), fondly called 'Baba Auwalu.' He was a Muslim convert, an apostle of the Lord Jesus Christ – full of the Spirit. He seemed to have been alone in a system that reeked of corruption, but the Lord was in and with Him, and that made all the difference. The dark forces that propelled the engines of corruption within the police force were subdued by the superior *huberballon megethos* power at work in him. He broke the levers that steered unrighteousness and made it a norm within the police force by lifting his hands continually in surrender to God!

What? You would have to excuse my shock because the Nigerian Police Force is known to be one of the most corrupt

205

institutions in Nigeria. Seeing a man not only standing for the Lord but building a service platform by which teenagers, toddlers, and adults were harvested into the kingdom of God in a police barracks (a place that was known to be a breeding ground for restive and varmint youth), was a scene of biblical proportion.

Many *barracks boys and girls* met the Lord through Hossana Goodnews Fellowship, and Baba Auwalu paid extreme prices to keep the fellowship going. He endured humiliation, marginalisation, being called unprintable names and gargantuan persecutions from parents, colleagues, and superiors, yet his words and deeds ministered grace. He stood for righteousness and refused to be a part of the institutional corruption that plagued the police force. So, for his entire career, his superiors knew he would not *play ball* when assigned to do duties that would breach his covenant with God. His superiors, colleagues, and juniors knew Baba Auwalu to be a *genuine pastor*. He was a faithful steward of the grace of God. His ministry reached out to families in the police force.

He passed away not long after I joined the fellowship, but I believe his legacy is written in gold in eternity. Hossana Good News Fellowship made my stay in Kano an adventure of a lifetime with God. My life and ministry were changed forever. During my time there, the Lord handed me the blueprint of my ministry and blessed me with relationships that are profitable to my life and ministry to date. There I saw first-hand the possibility of being God's apostle in the marketplace and how that it is possible to win by righteousness.

If God could raise an apostle and send him to the

Nigerian Police Force (generally considered to be a bastion of corruption) with great results, then He can send any believer to the darkest crevices of the marketplace with even greater results. Through Hossana Good News Fellowship, many have been raised in service of the Lord - I am talking about both within and outside the church. Great functionaries in the kingdom of God to the nations have risen through this platform - too numerous to mention by name here. Romans 10:18 captures the impact of this work perfectly,

> "Their sound has gone out to all the earth, and their words to the ends of the world." (Romans 10:18, NKJV)

Such is the testimony of all those who dare execute God's will in the portion of the marketplace allocated to them by God.

Dear God's apostle in the marketplace, this epistle has been written to let you know that you are God's epistle in the marketplace, to be read by all men in the world. God's refulgent light is trapped in your vessel. Give way and let your light so shine that the darkness in your domain of influence is chased into oblivion - to the glory of the Lord Jesus Christ. Someone once said, 'Men in the world do not read the Bible. They read your life. Ensure that each time they read you, you are turned to the right chapter.'

I close this book with a fiery poetic piece from my friend, Gideon Odoma, wherein he powerfully captures the urgency with which the gospel of the kingdom of our Lord Jesus Christ ought to be managed at every Christian soldier's duty post. This is even more serious for those who are stationed in the marketplace:

OF SPLENDOUR & RADIANCE: A gospel chant

Christian, beware. There is a stranded gospel. It is:
decaffeinated,
emasculated and
consequently deficient
in bite,
in power and
in the gospel's otherwise signature Tsunami.

This anaemic gospel that drawls and crawls and entreats people with famished importunities is a criminally impotent version of what Jesus secured for us by His stellar life and atoning, salvific work. May we never be found peddling such caricature of the real deal.

Punch and power are inescapable hallmarks of the true gospel of the true Christ. That's why I am not ashamed of the gospel of Christ. It is the power of God for salvation... and God calls us to be heralds of the gospel, a gospel sublime,

untameable,
free,
liberating,
profound,
unyielding, and
eternal.

Let's rise; rise to our ordination.

Inherent in the gospel of Christ is an avalanche
of celestial dynamite,
of stupendous brilliance, and
of the combined radiance of the sunbeams of a thousand

The gospel of Christ
reels with wonder,
is resplendent in majesty,
is pungent in power.

More powerful than anything 'power' could ever mean.

I take my place here as a privileged herald in a long line of endowed handlers of the conquering mystery called the gospel. The Holy fires that differentiated and distinguished previous generations of my fore-bearers in this sacred enterprise, the fire that set them apart from feeble professors of a beggarly sort of gospel has been pleased to ignite my ravished heart. I speak of the holy flames of the thrice-holy God. I am His.

Holy, Holy, Holy is the Lord God almighty!

Holy!

The Lord's wisdom and power multiply in you as you take on the portion of the marketplace allocated to you by Him in His name!

YOU ARE NOT OUTNUMBERED: THE MAJORITY OF ONE WITH GOD!

OTHER BOOKS BY THE AUTHOR
AROME OSAYI

IF YOU HAVE BEEN BLESSED BY GODWARD YOU WILL LOVE THESE...

PLEASE VISIT YOUR LOCAL BOOKSTORE.
OR www.ironpenbooks.net TO PLACE YOUR ORDER